Kristin & Sarah —
Be Friends

**Straight
Talk
for Girls**

From Dad! —

Other Books for Teens by Bill Sanders

Straight
Talk
for Girls

BILL SANDERS

Fleming H. Revell
A Division of Baker Book House Co
Grand Rapids, Michigan 49516

© 1995 by Bill Sanders

Published by Fleming H. Revell
a division of Baker Book House Company
P.O. Box 6287, Grand Rapids, MI 49516-6287

Fifth printing, June 2001

Printed in the United States of America

Library of Congress Cataloging-in-Publication Data

Sanders, Bill, 1951–
    Straight talk for girls / Bill Sanders.
       p.   cm.
    ISBN 0-8007-5577-4 (pbk.)
    1. Teenage girls—Religious life. 2. Teenage girls—Conduct of life. 3. Christian life—Juvenile literature. I. Title.
BV4551.2.S26   1995
248.8′33—dc20   95-34251

Unless otherwise marked, Scripture quotations are from the New American Standard Bible, © the Lockman Foundation 1960, 1962, 1963, 1968, 1971, 1972, 1973, 1975, 1977.

Scripture quotations marked NIV are from the HOLY BIBLE, NEW INTER-NATIONAL VERSION®. NIV®. Copyright © 1973, 1978, 1984 by International Bible Society. Used by permission of Zondervan Publishing House. All rights reserved.

Scripture quotations marked TLB are from *The Living Bible,* copyright © 1971 by Tyndale House Publishers, Wheaton, Illinois. Used by permission.

For current information about all releases from Baker Book House, visit our web site:
              http://www.bakerbooks.com/

Contents

Introduction

Join me on an adventure into the mind, heart, and soul. In these pages we'll start a voyage to discover who the awesome Creator really is and meet with the One who is our heavenly Father and wants to be our guide.

This will also be an expedition of trust. You see, I'm on this trip too, and in the process I'm learning to totally lean on God. Though I'm not there yet, I've only a lifetime to go. I don't understand God fully, but I still trust and love him and can honestly say that everything good that has ever come into my life has come from him.

Becoming part of this expedition requires the honesty that goes hand in hand with trust. Like me, you may find that being straight with God isn't nearly as hard as being honest with yourself. In keeping with that honesty, in this book I've sometimes clearly revealed my own lack of faith—including the questions I hardly know how to ask and the answers I have yet to find. I want to respect you by showing you the whole range of faith—including the unanswered questions.

Maybe this book will raise a lot of questions in your life—and maybe we won't find all the answers. But if that leads you to fall in love with our one, true God with every fiber of your being, to trust him when you don't understand, and to count on him to come through for you, I will have achieved my greatest aim.

Living the way God directs us is better by far—even on its worst days—than going the way of the world. Though my words may fail at times, I want you to understand how much your heavenly Father wants to be with you all the way—for the rest of your life.

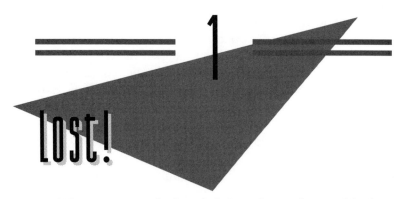

1

Lost!

When you were a little girl, did you have a favorite blankie, teddy, doggy, or something else that you slept with? Most of us had something special—many junior-high, high-school, or even college students have a favorite stuffed animal.

I remember the day, when I was five, that I went to the store to get Smokie the Bear. I still have him, though I don't sleep with him. (Oh, sure, maybe a nap now and then.) He's still very special to me.

For my daughter Emily, it's bunnies. We've had at least one bunny in our family since her very first Christmas. They are small, the size of your hand, and made of the softest material you can imagine. In our cedar chest, for safekeeping, lies Emily's very first bunny, held together by threads at the places where she has loved all the stuffing out of it. Four more yellow and pink bunnies—just like the first—have replaced it. The more they are loved, hugged, held tight, and rolled over at night, the more they look like the original bunny. Hardly a night has passed in eleven years when my daughter hasn't had them close by.

But recently, for two days and nights, we searched high and low for those bunnies, and they were nowhere to be found. On the second night, as I was about to say prayers with Emily, she remembered exactly where they were. A desperate expression of worry, fright, and terror covered her face as she realized the fate of her friends. "They took them away!" she half shouted.

"What do you mean?" I asked. "Who took them away?"

"The junk people—when they took the stuff from our garage! I put them in the little picnic basket you tried to throw away. Now I'll never see them again!" As she ran downstairs to tell her mom, I realized that I had put the old picnic basket back in the garage after she had rescued it from the junk pile.

Later, rubbing Emily's back to get her to calm down and go to sleep, I promised her I would get the bunnies back. When I went to bed that night, all I could think of was making a call and driving wherever I had to go to rummage through anything to find that basket.

First thing in the morning, I made the call. I was relieved when the woman on the other end of the line said, "The guys haven't gone through Saturday's stuff yet; you may still be in luck."

I drove straight to the junkyard. As I told the men there (who looked meaner than any junkyard dogs) what I was after, they chuckled, as if to say, "What's the big deal about some little bunnies?"

That's when it hit me: I didn't care if the whole town's population laughed; I was going to find those little pieces of cloth if it was the last thing I did. I deeply loved my little girl and was going to do all I could to make her happy.

As I looked to my right, on top of a large pile of suitcases and boxes, there it was. I grabbed the basket with the excitement of a six-year-old on Christmas morning and quickly peeked inside to find four of the most beautiful things I've ever seen in my life: the bunnies.

I couldn't wait to see Emily's face when she came home from school and looked at, held, and hugged her lost friends.

Even though it took a lot of effort, I'm glad I could find the bunnies for Emily. It's rare that I go to that much trouble for anything, and my willingness to do it showed my love for her.

Of course, when I start thinking about love, I can't avoid thinking about God. Sometimes I'm like Emily. I lose track of the One I love, or worse, I simply lose interest. So I have to ask myself some questions about the kind of love I show God.

Why don't I get as excited about digging into his Word each morning as I was about finding the bunnies? He has plenty to say about the particular questions or problems I have in my life.

How glad I am that God searched for me for twenty-eight years as I purposely hid from him (unlike the bunnies, who had nothing to say about it). "Look! I have been standing at the door and I am constantly knocking. If anyone hears me calling him and opens the door, I will come in and fellowship with him and he with me" (Rev. 3:20 TLB).

> No matter how far I get
> from the center
> of God's will, he never
> gives up on me.

Why was God willing to keep going the distance for me? He was compelled by the same reason I wanted to find and return Emily's bunnies: He loved me and wanted to make me happy. "For God so loved the world, that He gave His only begotten Son, that whoever believes in Him should not perish, but have eternal life" (John 3:16).

When I'm alone and scared in a big, dark world, even though it may seem that God is nowhere to be found, I need to keep looking for him. After all, he promised, "When you pray, I will listen. You will find me when you seek me, if you look for me in earnest" (Jer. 29:12–13 TLB).

Searching for Emily's bunnies taught me some good lessons about my commitment to God. I need to put in the effort it takes to find answers to tough questions. When I do it God's way and take the trouble, I get the answers I'm looking for.

No matter how far I get from the center of God's will, he never gives up on me. Because he loves me, he keeps searching for me—and he'll do the same for you too. "For the Lord God says: I will search and find my sheep. I will be like a shepherd looking for his flock. I will find my sheep and rescue them from all the places they were scattered in that dark and cloudy day. And I will bring them back" (Ezek. 34:11–13 TLB).

God shouldn't have to look far for me. I want to be the first one back in his arms! Hope to see you there!

2
More Than Turkey Day

Last fall as I was turning on the heat in my cottage, preparing to hibernate for four days and write another book, a sharp, burning pain stabbed my heart. Each effort to fill my lungs felt as though I was being tortured by a blacksmith's red-hot steel poker. Five painful steps brought me to my chair, and I eased myself down, concentrating on remaining perfectly still.

The pain didn't go away, and I couldn't breathe. "I'm going to die," I realized.

"Breathe slower." My thoughts sped on helter-skelter.

"Why can't I calm down?"

"But I can't die," my mind objected. "I had a fight with the kids this morning, and we left mad. I never said, 'I love you.'"

"Why can't I pray? God help me. I've got to get to the phone. But I'll die if I move!"

All I could do was sit extremely still, desperately frightened, looking ahead. Three feet in front of me stood our wall-sized bulletin board covered with ten years' worth of pictures. My life didn't have to flash before my eyes—it was smack-dab in front of me.

Holding my side with my forearm, I beheld mountains of memories—and they brought on mixed emotions and confusion. There was my best friend and wife, Holly, cooking, swimming, and skiing. My kids were there—and I knew I'd never have a chance to say "Good-bye," "I love you," or "I'm sorry; please forgive me." My mom and dad stood there too. "I'm never going to be with them again." My mind would not let up. "How can I get to that phone? I've got to say good-bye to Holly. Even if it kills me, I must try."

Despite the pain, feeling as if I would die, I kept on trying to reach the phone. I never actually prayed, "Dear God, please let me see my family again. Give me one last chance to make things right—to give more hugs and model my love for you more consistently." But thoughts like that recurred time and again.

After making my way to the phone, I called Holly and told her in a faint voice that I thought I was having a heart attack. Then I called 911. The coming sirens sounded louder than any I'd ever heard before—then they became fainter. Realizing they were lost, I called again and gave more exact directions so the ambulance could find its way around the lake's unmarked roads.

During my first ambulance ride, the emergency medical team took an EKG and told me I was not having a heart attack.

Thank you, God!

After I was checked into the hospital, Holly came through the door, worry written all over her face. She walked over and took my hand. I'll never be able to explain it, but the pain totally disappeared as she held my hand. As quickly as it had come, it left me.

No one may be able to explain my mysterious "heart attack," but I am thankful for it because I know it gave me a new heart. That terrible experience taught me a lot about thanksgiving. I'm not just talking about Turkey Day, either.

I realized how much I have to be thankful for when I thought I'd never have the chance to appreciate the people I love most. Saying "Thank you" and "I love you" means a lot more to me today than it used to.

You see, I'd become too complacent and rushed. My heart attitude wasn't focused on the most important things. I needed to give more hugs rather than excuses for why I was too busy to do so. And I needed to slow down and give thanks where it was due—to God and to other people.

Now my heart has a new prayer. It goes like this:

> Thank you, God, for giving me my family and friends and another chance to enjoy them. Amen.

3

What Do You Lack?

Do you feel as if you are lacking something? You know—as if you're missing an important part, haven't got it right yet, or just can't make the grade. Did you also know that description doesn't fit you if you know Jesus?

How do I know? It's because the last thing Jesus said on the cross was "It is finished!" (John 19:30). He meant that his work was complete. Paul follows that up by saying, "In Him [Jesus] you [believers in Jesus] have been made complete" (Col. 2:10).

People attempt to fill the void by trying to get the world to notice them. They feel empty, worthless, and useless unless things, people, and positive circumstances make them feel good inside. Or they become more assertive and work hard trying to believe in themselves. But they are on the wrong track, because they'll never find completeness in clothes, toys, prestige, or fame.

Paul warns Christians: "See to it that no one takes you captive through hollow and deceptive philosophy, which depends on human tradition and the basic principles of this world rather than on Christ" (Col. 2:8–10 NIV). Paul doesn't want us to fall for something that looks solid on the surface but is really empty, blank, and useless—hollow. Nor should we fall for the false, deceitful, misleading, and unreal philosophies the world has to offer. These depend on the unwritten laws, customs, and practices of human tradition.

The world teaches:

- Believe in yourself.
- Assert yourself.
- Be independent.
- More is better.
- Demand attention.

That's exactly the kind of hollow and deceptive philosophy Paul was talking about. To follow God, simply ignore those teachings and

- believe in God.
- submit yourself.
- be interdependent.
- don't gain the world by losing your soul.
- serve others.

The first list is followed by people looking to make the most of this world; the second is a guide for those looking toward a heavenly world. Did you notice that they are direct opposites? So are the results of following them.

If you want the complete world of God instead of the empty, foolish philosophies of this world, realize that you can never be complete in an incomplete world. You'll only be whole in Jesus. That's why I wrote a kind of unusual Christmas list to Jesus in the form of a letter.

Dear Jesus,
Because I am complete in you:

1. *I do not need to believe in me, to be perfect, making myself my own God.* Since you are God, and I am the worshiper, you go on being perfect and I'll go on being

human. With your help, I'll try my best, and when I fall, I'll grab on to you.

I won't be like your greatest angel, who let his desire to be God destroy him when he said, "I will ascend to heaven; I will raise my throne above the stars of God, and I will sit on the mount. . . . I will make myself like the Most High" (Isa. 14:13–14; see also Luke 14:11; 18:11; 1 Tim. 3:6).

2. *I do not need to be noticed.* I want others to see you in me, not me. Like John, I proudly and confidently say, "[You] must increase, but I must decrease" (John 3:30; see also James 3:16).

3. *I do not need to be served or waited on.* I want to follow in your steps—washing others' feet; meeting their needs; looking for problems to solve, hurts to mend, frowns to turn upside down. "As each one has received a special gift, employ it in serving one another" (1 Peter 4:10; see also Matt. 20:28; Rom. 7:6; Gal. 5:13).

4. *I do not need any thing, activity, or person who would take my mind off you.* Please help me get rid of my need to spend time making myself look good. Help me spend less time on my hobbies, work, or time with friends if any of these take me away from you (see Rom. 8:6–7; Col. 3:2; 1 Tim. 6:7–8). Help me put aside time to

- be with my family—laughing, having fun worshiping you through our abundant life.
- prepare my heart on Saturday night for my worship time on Sunday.
- have a quiet, special time with you each day.
- read your Word and study your answer book.
- ask what you would do in difficult situations instead of doing what makes me feel good.

5. *I do not need to worry about anything.* If you and I can handle it, we will. If not, it's yours totally. "They are choked with worries and riches and pleasures of this life,

and bring no fruit to maturity" (Luke 8:14; see also 1 Peter 5:7).

6. *I do not fear.* Help me be so excited about my new life in you that fear is a thing of the past. With you on my side, why should I be afraid of anything or anyone? "The LORD is my light and my salvation; whom shall I fear?" (Ps. 27:1). "There is no fear in love; but perfect love casts out fear" (1 John 4:18).

Merry Christmas, Jesus.

I love you.

Bill

Knowing Jesus means you have all these gifts every day of the year, not simply on December 25. You can live in his strength 365 days a year! So what are you lacking?

4
A Matter of Focus

People are pretty good, right? They are usually honest and helpful. You always look for the best in them—even when life isn't going your way. Don't you?

Well, maybe you don't. But if you look for the worst in people, you're pretty sure to find it.

What we experience in people—and in life—is a matter of attitude. You can see a half-full or a half-empty glass, build up friends and family or tear them down, smile or frown when you face troubles. It's your own choice.

Even being a Christian won't automatically turn your frown into a smile. That's why I got this letter a little while ago:

Dear Bill,

In the back of your book you said to write if we had a problem. Well, I do. I'm always sad, and I don't know what to do about it. I've been a Christian since sixth grade, and now I'm a senior. Someday I plan on being a missionary. But I'm always sad, and I want to change.

What can I do?

Marlene

Depression can come from lots of places, and Marlene needs to have a thorough physical exam to rule out the possibility of an illness or chemical imbalance that would make her sad. If that's the problem, her doctor can give her a lot of help.

But many people feel sad not due to a physical problem but because they're focusing on the negative and ignoring good things in their lives. Once I know nothing's medically wrong, I ask people these questions:

Are you focusing on God or on your problems? Even when you have a lot going for you, you may not see it if your eyes are looking in the wrong direction. God told Moses, "Send out for yourself men so that they may spy out the land of Canaan, which I am going to give to the sons of Israel" (Num. 13:2).

What had God just promised? "I *am* going to give this land to you." He didn't waffle or use the expressions "maybe," "perhaps," "I might someday," "there's a slim chance," "God willing" (after all, he was God, and he was willing), "weather permitting," or "in all likelihood." In his eyes, it was a done deal.

Twelve men went to look over the land. Ten were sad all the time—they never saw the glass as even half-full; it was almost empty, and the water was warm besides. The other two had a positive outlook. God had told them, and they believed him—period.

When it came time to make their reports, those attitudes showed up bright and clear. "Caleb quieted the people, . . . 'We should by all means go up and take possession of it, for we shall surely overcome it.' But the men who had gone up with him said, 'We are not able to go up against the people, for they are too strong for us'" (Num. 13:30–31).

The majority report was negative: "The land devours its inhabitants; and all the people . . . are men of great size. . . . We became like grasshoppers in our own sight, and so we were in their sight" (Num. 13:32–33).

Even God's promise didn't seem to outweigh their perceptions.

Are you focusing on the size of your problems or on the size of God? How easy we all find it to stare at our own circumstances rather than digging into our memories and recalling the great things God has done for us. When we feel down and out, we have a hard time remembering that God has never and will never lie to his children or leave them stranded.

Once Caleb made his report, Joshua chimed in: "The land . . . is an exceedingly good land. If the LORD is pleased with us, then He will bring us into this land and give it to us. . . . Only do not rebel against the LORD; and do not fear the people of the land, for they shall be our prey." Can you tell he's getting more confident as he focuses on the Lord? "Their protection has been removed from them, and the LORD is with us; do not fear them" (Num. 14:7–9).

Five words Joshua used should give us the edge on sadness, feeling sorry for ourselves, or having a negative attitude toward life: "The Lord is with us!"

> **Count your blessings and put them to use for God, and you won't have time or the inclination to feel sad. Life is too precious and exciting for you to sit back and avoid getting the most from it.**

Which men did the people of Israel listen to? The majority. The crowd turned pessimistic and angry: "But all the congregation said to stone them with stones. Then the glory of the LORD appeared. . . . And the LORD said to Moses, 'How long will this people spurn Me? And how long will they not believe in Me, despite all the signs I have performed in their midst?'" (Num. 14:10–11).

It doesn't take a great mind to recall the blessings God has already given us, but sometimes we choose not to remember. If we follow with the majority report—the negative one— like the Israelites, we may end up walking in circles in the desert for forty years.

Would you rather do laps than enter the Promised Land? That's what you'll get if you sing the blues in order to fit in with the majority. How much better to focus on the Lord and have the strength of the Creator of the universe to help you.

Are you obeying God? If you go with the majority, you'll follow the maxim "Take success, you deserve it." If you choose to be an individual and go against the flow, you won't follow that worldly message. Instead you'll rest in God's promise that if you give yourself for his name's sake, he will give you inner peace and blessings that the richest person on earth doesn't have.

Jesus described this kind of lifestyle to his followers:

> Humble men are very fortunate! . . . for the Kingdom of Heaven is given to them. Those who mourn are fortunate! for they shall be comforted. The meek and lowly are fortunate! for the whole wide world belongs to them.
>
> Happy are those who long to be just and good, for they shall be completely satisfied. Happy are the kind and merciful, for they shall be shown mercy. Happy are those whose hearts are pure, for they shall see God. Happy are those who strive for peace—they shall be called the sons of God. Happy are those who are persecuted because they are good, for the Kingdom of Heaven is theirs.
>
> When you are reviled and persecuted and lied about because you are my followers—wonderful! Be happy about it! Be very glad! for a tremendous reward awaits you in heaven. And remember, the ancient prophets were persecuted too.
>
> Matthew 5:3–12 TLB

Do you want to be comforted and happy? Are complete satisfaction and feelings of joy and peace your desire? You can reach such heights in life if you are willing to be called a friend of the Creator of the universe. (For ideas on how to be that, reread the verses we've just looked at.)

Have you given thanks for each and every blessing God's given you? Though Marlene wants to lead others to Christ, her life and attitude could make others want to hide from both her and the God she portrays. Who would want to follow someone who is miserable?

Even though I don't know her, I know Marlene has a lot to be thankful for. As a Christian:

- she is God's child.
- her sins have been completely taken care of. "You were dead in sins. . . . Then he gave you a share in the very life of Christ, for he forgave all your sins, and blotted out the charges proved against you" (Col. 2:13–14 TLB).
- heaven is her future home—she'll have a mansion, no less!
- she has her health: eyes, ears, heart, and mind that work normally. She can walk, talk, skip, and jump.
- she has freedom in a country where she can be whom she wants to be, go where she wishes, and do whatever she wants.
- she has a family. Marlene isn't homeless or living by herself under an overpass or in a cardboard box on the street of a large city. Someone is taking care of her—she may have a mom and dad who love her very much. If she gets sick, the best doctors will care for her. Each week she goes to a church full of believers, where she can worship God and learn more about him.
- people pray for her and care deeply about her. Many aren't related to her by blood, but they are by love.
- she has friends. When she feels sorry for herself, Marlene probably takes her eyes off her friends (it's a very natural thing to do). But there are some true-blue people who are always there for her. While she may be concentrating on the kids she *wishes* would be her friends, she's ignoring the people she already has.

If I knew Marlene, I could probably help her write down a lot more of the blessings God has given her. Everyone should have a blessed list with at least five hundred specific things God has provided. On that list should appear every health item, every friend, every talent, and every opportunity in her life.

Count your blessings and put them to use for God, and you won't have time or the inclination to feel sad. Life is too precious and exciting for you to sit back and avoid getting the most from it. Banish the blues by putting these ideas to work for you today.

5
A Family Fix

There's no doubt that families, as well as individuals, could use some fixing. Sometimes desperate teens write me about their serious family problems. Like this letter:

Dear Bill,
I am so full of confusion and anger over my family that I could just about burst!
My older brother who just dropped out of college has a mental illness. When he comes home, he controls and verbally abuses my mother. Recently he made her feel guilty when he told her that he'd be okay if she were a better mother.
I'm the levelheaded one in our family, and at sixteen, I'm the one she complains to when my brother goes on one of his rampages. But when it comes time to tell him he has to leave the house and stop abusing my mom, she takes his side and feels sorry for him.
What can I do to change her and fix my family?
Family Rescuer

I hope the response I gave her helps other teens who are in the same situation.

Dear Family Rescuer,

I'm so glad you've written me about a problem that plagues many people of all ages.

Trying to change a person is often futile because if they don't want the change to happen, it won't. Your mom sounds as if she's codependent, which means she feels she has to defend your brother and cover up for him. Her problems are probably pretty deep, and you will not be able to help her on your own, no matter how hard you try. So get help from someone older and wiser than you—preferably a professional counselor.

From someone who has been right where you are now, here are some tips.

Remember that you can't make others change, even if it is for their own good. Though you can pray for them and help them to the best of your abilities, unless they get some serious counseling or God changes them, a year from now they will remain just as they are today.

Release yourself from the role of rescuer. Rescuing others only prolongs the time it takes them to hit rock bottom, and God can help them only when they realize how helpless they are and turn to him.

If your mom continues to let your brother abuse her, he will never be forced to deal with his illness. You can't make your mom stand up for herself; that will only happen when she becomes sick and tired of the situation. When she kicks him out and he has to find out what it's like in the world, he'll quickly learn that others won't let him treat them the way he treats his guilt-ridden mom.

You can't do anything about this. Your family is dysfunctional, but you didn't cause it, and you can't fix it. Your mom and brother need professional help, but they'll have to want it and seek it. Stop rescuing and let God and the natural consequences take over.

Get counseling yourself so you can start to develop healthy expectations for yourself. Some of the things you may learn could include:

- It's okay to make mistakes; you don't have to be perfect. Nor do you have to meet everyone's needs.
- You can pray and do your best, but you will never make things perfect in your family.
- You will never get everyone's approval, so don't expect it. But don't worry, no one ever gets worldwide approval anyway.
- Though you sometimes let other people down, it's okay—you aren't God!
- You can and will have days when you need help yourself. That's okay too. It's healthy to need others and need God.
- Your mom and brother are choosing their own lives and must live with the consequences. Keep praying and let God take over.
- You have the right to get angry, but with God's help, you won't lose your cool. He can help you love your family even when they frustrate you with their actions.
- God is in charge and is stronger than you are. With God, all things are possible, and he's still in the miracle business. Turn your mom and brother over to him and enjoy your high-school years instead of becoming totally engulfed in their lives and poor choices.

Professional counseling can help you achieve all these things.

You can also start to change your way of thinking by committing yourself to God's way. This prayer can be a start:

Thank you, Lord, for always being with me and never leaving me alone. Instead of filling my mind with nothing but my family's problems, I'm going to think of the things you want on my mind: "Whatever is true, whatever is honorable, whatever is right, whatever is pure, whatever is lovely, whatever is of good repute, if there is any excellence and if anything worthy of praise, let your mind dwell on these things. . . . and the God of peace shall be with you" (Phil. 4:8–9). Amen.

God bless you.

Bill

6

I'm Not Everybody, and I'm Not Doing It!

"Everybody's doing it," you hear wherever you go. Whoever says it can be talking about premarital sex, drinking, doing drugs, being too busy to spend time with their family, or cheating on a test.

If you are tired of hearing those words, I've got great news for you. Everyone *isn't* doing it, and I want you to be proud to tell others, "I'm not everybody, and I'm not doing it."

When people send you that message, they're trying to tell you there's only one way to go. But the truth is that you get to choose whom you focus on, listen to, and model your life after. Remember, for every Dr. Ruth and supporter of Planned Parenthood, there is a Josh McDowell and Dr. James Dobson. For every powerful person wanting to legalize drugs, there are thousands more fighting to keep drugs out of our lives. For every man or woman of power who has no character, there are millions living God-fearing lives.

God's people aren't like everybody. Here are some who feared and loved God and didn't follow the crowd:

1. *Joseph* didn't have sex with another man's wife. When his master's wife enticed him, he turned her down with these words:

> "There is no one greater in this house than I, and he has withheld nothing from me except you, because you are his wife. How then could I do this great evil, and sin against God?" And it came about as she spoke to Joseph day after day, that he did not listen to her to lie beside her, or be with her.
>
> Genesis 39:9–10

If you haven't run into a boyfriend who can take Joseph's stand, maybe you haven't been looking in the right place— or maybe you've never been willing to challenge the guys you've dated to really live for Jesus.

2. An *unknown prophet* knew the meaning of obeying God even in seemingly insignificant areas like what to eat and drink:

> But the man of God said to the king, "If you were to give me half your house I would not go with you, nor would I eat bread or drink water in this place. For so it was commanded me by the word of the LORD, saying, 'You shall eat no bread, nor drink water, nor return by the way which you came.'"
>
> 1 Kings 13:8–9

3. Asked by the wicked king Ahaziah to take part in a sailing venture, *Jehoshaphat* said no to sin. "Then Ahaziah the son of Ahab said to Jehoshaphat, 'Let my servants go with your servants in the ships.' But Jehoshaphat was not willing" (1 Kings 22:49).

Christians can say no because they keep their eyes on Jesus. He was like us in all points except that he didn't give in to the temptation to sin. Keep your eyes on him.

> Since then we have a great high priest who has passed through the heavens, Jesus the Son of God, let us hold

fast our confession. For we do not have a high priest who cannot sympathize with our weaknesses, but one who has been tempted in all things as we are, yet without sin. Let us therefore draw near with confidence to the throne of grace, that we may receive mercy and may find grace to help in time of need.

Hebrews 4:14–16

The next time someone scoffs at your moral standards and says, "Come on, everybody's doing it," you know what to say and do.

Encourage yourself with this verse: "If sinners entice you, do not consent" (Prov. 1:10). You might even want to put that verse up on the inside of your locker!

7

The Miracle
Red Cleaner

I received a letter from a girl whose problem is not that uncommon:

Dear Bill,

I feel so dirty inside, and no matter how hard I try, I can't seem to get over it. Since I've done so many terrible things in my life, I don't know if God will ever love me or forgive me. I feel so ashamed of what I've done.

Please tell me, is there any hope for people like me?

Dirty and Ashamed

Do you ever feel dirty or ashamed or concerned about whether God could love you?

Sin is supposed to concern us and shake us up—not because we feel mad at ourselves for not doing better, but because we have sinned against a holy and loving God who deserves more from us. In this book, we'll talk a lot about sin and the way it destroys, kills, and separates. But let's start with a look at the way it stains us and makes us feel dirty.

When God talks about sin, he doesn't compare it to the dirt your favorite cleaner can wash out. He describes it as a permanent stain that only he can remove. Though we may try a lot of things to make the stain disappear—like being extra good for a few days or going to church twice as often—we still feel far away from God.

Sin is the only thing that can separate us from God: "But your iniquities have separated you from your God; your sins have hidden his face from you, so that he will not hear" (Isa. 59:2 NIV). When we sin, an invisible wall comes between us and God. Since God is light, it's no wonder we feel as if we're in the dark when we don't know that he is taking care of us and loving us.

The girl who wrote me felt the stain of sin. She knew that she'd done wrong, and the result of her wrongdoing spread across her life, causing her much pain. What she didn't know was that she was not alone in her predicament. God knew her problem. That's why he said, "Come now, let us reason together. . . . Though your sins are like scarlet, they shall be as white as snow; though they are red as crimson, they shall be like wool" (Isa. 1:18 NIV).

We are guilty, covered with a deep red stain. The scarlet color described in that verse refers to a potent dye obtained from a small worm found on the leaves of an oak tree in Mediterranean countries. Material was double dipped in the permanent dye.

Imagine that you had borrowed a one-of-a-kind, heirloom, pure white sweater from your best friend, who had received it from her great-great-aunt Hilda. While you are preparing to tie-dye some T-shirts, you drop the sweater into a permanent red dye.

"It's ruined," you cry. But you still do your best, washing the sweater forty times. The best you can get is pink.

"How am I going to explain pink?" you wonder. Of course you could try saying, "Are you sure it was white?" when your friend asks what happened. Maybe you could respond, "Can you say with absolute certainty that it was white when I got it from you the other day?" But you know those ploys won't work. What can you do?

Then a friend tells you of a stain remover that's absolutely too good to be true. It really works! The worse the stain, the better it cleans.

"Oh," you respond, "it probably costs too much."

Your friend gives you the greatest news in the world, "It's free to anyone who will take it. All you have to do is be truly sorry for dropping the sweater into the water and tell that to the owner of the stain remover."

You'd jump at the chance, wouldn't you?

But first you ask about the color of this fantastic, too-good-to-be-true stain remover. "It's red," your friend answers.

"Red! How will that change the color of the sweater?" you demand. Suspicious, you continue, "And why doesn't it cost anything? Everything costs something!"

Your friend answers, "It works—and it doesn't cost anything because it's already been paid for in full."

The permanent red stains of sin in our lives can be removed by the miracle red cleaner of Jesus' blood. "If we confess our sins, he is faithful and just and will forgive us our sins and purify us from all unrighteousness" (1 John 1:9 NIV). Though red blood might not seem the ideal cleanser, God promises, "Jesus Christ, who is the faithful witness, the firstborn from the dead, and the ruler of the kings of the earth . . . loves us and has freed us from our sins by his blood" (Rev. 1:5 NIV).

"Does it work on its own? Do I have to do anything?" you may wonder. God replies, "You must have faith in him, that's all. The price has already been paid." That's why Romans 3:25 says, "God presented him [Jesus] as a sacrifice of atonement, through faith in his blood" (NIV).

"Then why doesn't the girl who wrote that letter feel better?" you might want to know.

Perhaps she isn't aware of the miracle stain remover that requires only faith and repentance to clean our hearts. Or she may have been cleansed by God but doesn't really believe in it. Either way, she can start to feel clean once she puts 1 John 1:9 to work by confessing her sin before Jesus and turning from it. He's better than Molly Maid because he goes from heart to heart instead of from door to door.

Call him now for your free cleaning.

8
Abortion Rights and Wrongs

To avoid hearing about abortion rights, you'd have to be hiding under a rock. It's in the news and in plenty of conversations. That's why I wasn't surprised to get this letter.

Dear Bill,
  I am all for women having equal rights in the workplace. Don't you feel it's also perfectly normal for a woman to want to be in charge of her own body and be the one to decide whether or not she wants an abortion?
                                                    Equally Right

Whether or not she knows it, Equally Right agrees with all the feminist philosophies of right and wrong. *Rights* in this context means "the ability to do what I want."

But standing on your rights can be so wrong. You see, God didn't only create rights, he also created the word *wrong*. And whether you like it or not, God says abortion is wrong.

The Bible shows us that God has definite opinions on right and wrong. That's why he gave us the Ten Commandments, not the Ten Suggestions. In them, he clearly states his view: "You shall not murder" (Deut. 5:17).

Proverbs 6 provides a list of seven things God hates most. One of them is "hands that shed innocent blood" (v. 17).

"But having an abortion isn't murder," Equally Right might object.

That's not what God says. Through the psalmist's prayer, the Creator of all things says it pretty clearly:

> You made all the delicate, inner parts of my body, and knit them together in my mother's womb. Thank you for making me so wonderfully complex! It is amazing to think about. Your workmanship is marvelous—and how well I know it. You were there while I was being formed in utter seclusion! You saw me before I began to breathe. Every day was recorded in your Book!
>
> Psalm 139:13–16 TLB

God knew us while we were still in our mothers' wombs, and we were people even before we were born. Before he was born, John the Baptist jumped in his mother's womb with excitement at the news that Mary was carrying Jesus. "And it came about that when Elizabeth heard Mary's greeting, the baby leaped in her womb; and Elizabeth was filled with the Holy Spirit" (Luke 1:41).

Whether you like it or not, God says abortion is wrong.

Many abortions are done when the mother is six, seven, or eight months pregnant—and some of those children could have lived. What's the difference between those babies and ones to be born in one or two weeks? If the babies who will be born in a few weeks are children, why aren't those who were killed at six, seven, or eight months?

Equally Right is supporting something that is wrong—dead wrong. Having equal rights in the workplace does not give a woman the right to kill her child.

You see, when it comes to God's Word, everything else isn't equally right.

9
Amazing What?

Have you ever received something good that you didn't deserve?

You can answer yes to that question if you are a Christian, because God has given you grace. "For it is by grace you have been saved, through faith—and this not from yourselves, it is the gift of God—not by works, so that no one can boast" (Eph. 2:8–9 NIV).

"What does that mean?" you ask. "I still don't know what *grace* is."

I just heard a beautiful way to remember what it is. It's an acrostic:

God's
Redemption
At
Christ's
Expense

John Newton described it with the words:

> Amazing grace, how sweet the sound
> that saved a wretch like me.
> I once was lost but now am found,
> was blind, but now I see.

Another term for grace is *unmerited favor*, a fancy phrase for "approval you didn't deserve." God saved us because of his goodness and love for us. He didn't have to do it, and we certainly didn't earn it—that's grace.

Ephesians 2:8–9 says grace is not of ourselves but from God. We can't earn it by doing the right thing. So no matter how much you pray, give money to the poor, feed the hungry, clothe the naked, visit the prisoners and sick, love your neighbor, give tithes to the church, help others, become a servant to all people, and honor your parents, you can't buy your way into heaven.

That doesn't mean you shouldn't do all those good works. God calls you to do them. But unless you accept his free gift, even regularly doing all those things won't get you a place in heaven.

If your own efforts could open heaven's gates, you'd have a reason to boast in yourself. That would make you proud—something God doesn't want you to be. In fact, he promises to visit the humble and resist the proud (see James 4:6).

The New Testament often talks about being like a child. Have you ever taken care of a baby? She desperately needs her parents to take care of her. The other day I babysat for some friends' newborn baby. At a month and a half, little Madeline was so helpless I had to support her neck, or her head would flop around, and she'd be hurt. She choked on her bottle, and I had to pull it out of her mouth, sit her up, and burp her. She was totally dependent on me; her life was in my hands.

God wants us to be like Madeline—to totally need him. But we'd rather show off and let others know how great we are. As soon as we start to think, "You need me, don't you, God?" or, "Wow, this world sure is a better place because I'm around," we've gotten outside the bounds of grace and are trying to make ourselves into something. We become bragging and boastful, and God will oppose us.

Try bragging around your friends, and see how long they last. Show them your press releases, and you'll watch them disappear. I know it works that way because it's happened to me. Finally some people I loved got in my face and told me about it.

Though I don't know if he is a brother in Christ, I admire Michael Jordan's ability to accept things in a humble way. He's not like so many superstars who can't stop building themselves up. Notice that people don't applaud the proud stars as they do Michael Jordan because none of us appreciates arrogance.

Accept the gift of salvation from God and be thankful for it, knowing you could never earn it. Your attitude will make you a light in the world for others to follow.

Don't try to light up your own marquee. Give God the applause and win crowns for him by leading other people home toward him with you. The eternal rewards will be worth it.

10
Castle Busters

During a vacation in Fort Myers, Florida, my family and I learned a valuable lesson about discipline (or should I say the lack of it?). We'd just spent about two hours building a great sand castle with many small towers and about a hundred trees (a secret forest) around it. We looked up to find a boy about eight and a girl of three wanting to play with us.

"You can play right over here beside it and build one yourself," I offered.

They sat down, but soon they began inching closer and closer toward our masterpiece. A moment later I caught the boy smashing several of our sand trees.

"Don't do that!" I warned.

His mother, sitting on a beach blanket about fifteen feet from us, said nothing. Finally the boy moved a few feet away, at my insistence.

My family decided to go into the water. When we returned, the little demolition man had destroyed almost all the trees. We told him to leave, and reluctantly, he did.

A few minutes later, when we returned from throwing the Frisbee, we noticed he had ruined everything. My kids were heartbroken and angry. They wanted me to confront his parents and make certain the boy was punished.

I told my kids that apparently his parents don't discipline, since they had seen what happened when he menaced us earlier and had done nothing. "When you say something like that to many people, they react violently," I explained. "I don't care to get shot on the beach or followed back to our room by an angry dad."

In real life, people can be like that little demolition man too. Adults or teens may not ruin sand castles, but they can destroy the hopes and dreams of others.

Do you rip down emotional sand castles, or do you build them? Do you give people hope or rip it out of their hearts? When you walk out the door, are people glad to see you go, or do they wish you would stay?

Many people think I should have given that child's dad a piece of my mind, but what could it have proved? I asked myself, "What would Jesus have done?" Instead of confronting angry parents, I chose to teach my children a lesson on how to treat others. I also taught them that others don't have the right to make us upset—unless we give it to them. Jesus says we should pity wrongdoers, pray for them, turn the other cheek, and walk away (see Matt. 5:44; Luke 6:27–29).

Every day we run into destroyers. "Their feet run to evil, and they hasten to shed innocent blood; their thoughts are thoughts of iniquity; devastation and destruction are in their highways" (Isa. 59:7). Look out for people who tear apart ideas and plans, because life is full of them. When you run into them, try to find and bring out the good that is in them. If they insist on destroying and tearing down, move over and build your work of art on a different part of the beach.

11

Small Change

"I've tried to change over and over, and it just doesn't seem to work," Donna's discouragement bubbled over in words. "I know the things I say hurt people terribly, but I can't seem to stop. What am I doing wrong?"

Even though you know you've done something wrong and hurt others, change may come hard to you. But you are not alone. Lots of people have a hard time starting over. That's why many still struggle in their forties or fifties with problems that started in their teens: alcoholism, laziness, taking advantage of others, lying, stealing, spending money unwisely, sexual addiction. . . . The list could go on almost endlessly and include every problem people have known.

Good news! You can change if you are willing to learn the secret of turning old lifestyles and bad habits into new, healthy ones. Even though about 90 percent of the world struggles with the same old difficulties, you can stand apart if you want to.

My secret isn't difficult or hard to understand. It is:

DON'T DO IT ALONE!

To move in a new direction, you'll require strength and power above your own. You can have those through a renewal of your spirit by faith in Jesus Christ.

God described this extraordinary power to change: "Therefore, if anyone is in Christ, he is a new creation; the old has gone, the new has come!" (2 Cor. 5:17 NIV). Even though you may not feel as if you have it, God's power is right there with you.

Being "in Christ" means you are a born-again believer and are walking with him. Once you've committed your life to him, you have two advantages that are described in this verse. First, you are already new. God has given you what it takes to change—a new spirit. He's built the power right into you. Second, he's taken away the old you—the nature that wanted only to please Satan. Now you can do what pleases God and is good for you and others. Sin no longer has any power over you, and you don't have to obey it anymore. Call on Jesus whenever you need help, and he will be there.

"I may have a new nature and God's power," Donna commented, "but it sure is easy to sin anyway. I don't feel the power in me, at times, even though I know Jesus is there."

"Maybe you've let God's power get dusty and covered with cobwebs at the back of your heart," I suggested. "Thousands of Christians spend fifty times more hours choosing their wardrobes than they spend with the Power of the universe who resides in their own hearts.

"The old nature is gone, and so is Satan's grip on your life, but you must claim the new nature and live it, or it will remain a stranger to you," I explained. "God has already given you the power you'll need. He told you that the new has come. You can change—but maybe you don't really want to!" I challenged her.

Like Donna, millions of Christians complain that they are too weak to make the changes they'd like to see in their lives. Most of them simply don't recognize what God has already given them. They are new, and the Creator of the universe is theirs. He will never leave them or let them stay in a destructive lifestyle, but they must be willing to call on him and let him make the changes.

"You can't change all on your own," I pointed out to Donna.

"Don't I know it!"

"But you've got to stop trying to do it alone. As long as you struggle along under your own power, you're subconsciously saying there is no new strength in you and that even if there is, you won't use it." Then I shared the steps she needed to take.

"Identify the area in your life that you want changed."

"It's my mouth. . . . I need to say the right thing, not mess up all the time."

"Okay, now what do you want to replace that with? What would please God?"

"I guess I should be an encourager instead of someone who's always complaining or tearing people down."

"You'll have to figure out a step-by-step plan to achieve that goal. Look deep inside yourself," I told her, "and you will find that you know what to do." We talked it over for a while and came up with a few simple steps.

"My prayer life has been pretty stinky lately," Donna admitted. "I guess I should talk to God about my mouth every day. That'd be a good start."

"What are the attitudes that get you in trouble, and what ones do you need, Donna?" I prodded.

"Anger's my biggest downfall." She looked embarrassed as she told me. "I guess I need to see what God has to say on the subject." Donna perked right up as she realized, "That means I have to read my Bible, right?"

Before long, we had a list of Scripture verses that could support Donna in her lifestyle change.

"More prayer, I guess." Donna sighed. "Well, you didn't say it wouldn't take any effort, did you?"

"No, but if you keep on doing what's right and depending on God for strength, you can make the change. It's only when you start relying on yourself that you'll get into trouble," I warned her. "Pray every day and ask God to fill you. That way, if you do fall back into sin, you will hate it, because you'll know it doesn't please him.

"Love him with all your heart, mind, and soul. Praise him. Change will not only come, but it will stay," I promised.

If you know Jesus, you can take the same steps to intiate change in your life. Every time Satan knocks on your door, let Jesus answer, and someday Satan will just give up knocking.

12
Deny Myself?

"I'm supposed to love myself and think I'm not so hot all at the same time. I'm so confused," said seventeen-year-old Sarah.

I understood what she was talking about, and Sarah has a point. On the one hand, she's heard that she is made in God's image and should love the person she sees in the mirror. On the other hand, she's been taught to deny herself and put serving others before her own pleasures. Both messages are in the Bible—but how do you find a balance between them?

"But put on the Lord Jesus Christ, and make no provision for the flesh in regard to its lusts" (Rom. 13:14). As a Christian you can't live any way you want, and that means you have to deny yourself. But that doesn't mean you can't do anything that's enjoyable or that you have to be a doormat.

The apostle Paul denied himself a lot to spread the faith. He was ridiculed, chased out of towns, and sometimes feared for his life. You might think a man would have turned into a mouse after facing all that criticism. But no one could accuse Paul, who stood up to rulers and fractious churches, of being a wimp. He knew how to stand up for himself and Christ. Paul could deny himself and feel good about himself too because he had a higher goal than simple self-denial:

For this reason I endure all things for the sake of those who are chosen, that they also may obtain the salvation which is in Christ Jesus and with it eternal glory. It is a trustworthy statement: For if we died with Him, we shall also live with Him.

2 Timothy 2:10–11

Being a Christian means you give up some things, not so you can glory in your own humility, but so that you can show people what it means to know Christ and live for him. With the power of Jesus behind you, you have an inner confidence and strength that are not doormat material.

Denying yourself means you don't give in to sinful desires and mistreat your body by using drugs and alcohol or engaging in sex. Instead you serve others, as Jesus did when he washed the disciples' feet at the Last Supper.

Senselessly denying yourself anything you like to do is not going to gain you points in heaven. For the Christian, denial has a goal: "All things are lawful, but not all things are profitable. All things are lawful, but not all things edify. Let no one seek his own good, but that of his neighbor" (1 Cor. 10:23–24). Loving your neighbor as yourself will bring profit to the kingdom of God. Choosing the breakfast you least like because you think that will please God will not bring much profit.

> **God made you, and he wants you to feel great about yourself. Then, because you know and serve Jesus, you can focus on others and lead them to the God who made them.**

God's not out to be the heavenly killjoy. Nor is he saying that you need to feel unhappy in order to be holy. God made you, and he wants you to feel great about yourself. Then, because you know and serve Jesus, you can focus on others and lead them to the God who made them.

When you have to turn the other cheek as someone makes fun of you for being a Christian, know that your self-denial will only last for a while. "Yet a little while and the wicked man will be no more; and you will look carefully for his place, and he will not be there" (Ps. 37:10). Evil will not be glorified forever. God promised that in the ultimate reckoning, you will be glad you denied yourself: "Blessed are the gentle, for they shall inherit the earth" (Matt. 5:5).

Helping people know Jesus and inheriting the earth someday—aren't they goals worth a little self-denial?

13

Experience Is a Rough Teacher

Worried parents wrote to Ann Landers about their sixteen-year-old daughter who sneaked out to date an eighteen-year-old drug dealer. The parents were at their wits' end because they couldn't keep her under lock and key for the rest of her life, but they didn't want her to ruin her life either.

Ann advised them to get professional counseling. If that did not work, they would have to let their daughter go. She'd have to learn by experience.

Ann was right—parents can't hold on forever. But I feel for that girl if she doesn't listen to a counselor. Experience can be a rough teacher.

Some people will try to tell you that experience is the best teacher. They'll say, for example, that men and women should sleep together before they marry in order to find out if they are compatible. But they ignore the fact that none of us are shoes to be tried on before we're bought. A bad experience can hurt you deeply, and the pain may go on and on.

You don't have to experience all the evil in this world in order to learn what works best. God has already thought these things through and has written them down for you so you can avoid them. He frequently warns us against ignoring his commands and describes the benefits that faithfulness offers:

> I spoke to you in your prosperity;
> But you said, "I will not listen!"
> This has been your practice from your youth,
> That you have not obeyed My voice. . . .
> Then you will surely be ashamed and humiliated
> Because of all your wickedness.
>
> Jeremiah 22:21–22

> In spite of all this they still sinned,
> And did not believe in His wonderful works.
> So He brought their days to an end in futility,
> And their years in sudden terror.
>
> Psalm 78:32–33

> He who diligently seeks good seeks favor,
> But he who searches after evil, it will come to him.
>
> Proverbs 11:27

> For they cannot sleep unless they do evil;
> And they are robbed of sleep unless they make someone stumble.
> For they eat the bread of wickedness,
> And drink the wine of violence.
>
> Proverbs 4:16–17

> And this is the judgment, that the light is come into the world, and men loved the darkness rather than the light; for their deeds were evil. For everyone who does evil hates the light, and does not come to the light, lest his deeds should be exposed.
>
> John 3:19–20

People pay a heavy price if they don't learn from experience that sin is wrong. Don't let your friends draw you down the wide, painful path of sin because it will never be worth it. You will only find trouble.

Listen instead to the One who designed you, and lean on him. He's got a whole world of experience!

14

From Imperfect Father to Perfect Father

She had been abused, her life was in shambles, and her family was torn apart—all because of her own father. At this low point, a very wise person advised her, "Get a perfect father to help you love and understand your not-so-perfect father." That adviser was talking about her heavenly Father—God.

None of us have perfect parents. How do we forgive them for not being good to us or purposefully hurting us? What if their own pain and lack of self-control caused them to harm us?

Were our parents inflicted with pain as children? If so, they may think an abusive home is normal. They may have no example of a loving, Christian home with which to compare their lifestyle.

Did God seem to be far from your parents' families when they grew up? If so, maybe they did not understand love and forgiveness. A huge load of hurt may bear down on their hearts.

It's hard to comprehend a father who hurts or ignores his child—until you know something about pain and perception. When people experience pain throughout life—be it a dysfunctional home, alcoholism, abuse, drugs, workaholism, uncontrolled rage, or whatever—they see themselves, God, and the world in a distorted fashion. They think life is ugly. People are basically bad and cruel, and God doesn't care. Therefore, the only important thing is to feel good at all costs. If it hurts others or themselves, that's okay because pain is all there is anyway.

If this sounds normal to you or your parents, I've got some important news for you: God isn't uncaring, and life doesn't have to be harsh. In his Word, which nourishes our hearts and souls, God has shown us who he is and what our lives can be.

Before we look at these life-giving words of God's, I need to make something very clear. If you have been abused, especially sexually abused, you were the victim and the *abuser* was the one who sinned. You did absolutely nothing wrong. You didn't cause the abuse. Stop blaming yourself—self-blame is one of Satan's greatest tools. The person who hurt you had no right to do what he did. He sinned and God will deal with him.

In this chapter we are talking about Christian love and forgiveness. But before you can truly forgive someone who harmed you deeply you must 1) understand that it's not your fault and 2) work through the healing process (a professional is needed in almost all sexual abuse cases). And remember, God will never leave your side.

Now let's take a look at God's advice:

A new commandment I give to you, that you love one another, even as I have loved you, that you also love one another.

John 13:34

Have this attitude in yourselves which was also in Christ Jesus, who, although He existed in the form of God, did not regard equality with God a thing to be grasped, but emptied Himself, taking the form of a bond-servant, and being made in the likeness of men. And being found in appearance as a man, He humbled Himself by becoming obedient to the point of death, even death on a cross.

Philippians 2:5–8

By this the love of God was manifested in us, that God has sent His only begotten Son into the world so that we might live through Him. In this is love, not that we loved God, but that He loved us and sent His Son to be the propitiation for our sins. Beloved, if God so loved us, we also ought to love one another.

1 John 4:9–11

God wants you to start a new love-, hope-, and joy-filled life. Look to him for the hard-to-find answers. Once you are filled with the love of Christ, you can easily pass it on. If you don't know him, love is foreign to you. How I wish all hurting, hopeless people could truly believe these God-given truths:

And He said to them, "You shall love the Lord your God with all your heart, and with all your soul, and with all your mind." This is the great and foremost commandment. The second is like it, "You shall love your neighbor as yourself."

Matthew 22:37–39

So then, while we have opportunity, let us do good to all men, and especially to those who are of the household of the faith.

Galatians 6:10

Now we who are strong ought to bear the weaknesses of those without strength and not just please ourselves. Let each of us please his neighbor for his good, to his edification.

Romans 15:1–2

But if your enemy is hungry, feed him, and if he is thirsty, give him a drink; for in so doing you will heap burning coals upon his head. Do not be overcome by evil, but overcome evil with good.

Romans 12:20–21

Knowing Jesus as your Lord and Savior frees you from sin, Satan, and death. It also frees you to forgive those who have not treated you as God wanted them to. Break the imperfect cycle of hate and wrong by living out God's words.

For you were called to freedom, brethren; only do not turn your freedom into an opportunity for the flesh, but through love serve one another. For the whole Law is fulfilled in one word, in the statement, "You shall love your neighbor as yourself." But if you bite and devour one another, take care lest you be consumed by one another.

Galatians 5:13–15

Show your imperfect father the love of your heavenly Father, and your dad may come to Christ and be saved. With God's help, all things are possible: "I can do all things through Him who strengthens me" (Phil. 4:13). Never give up hope, but cling tightly to the truth. As you speak it, learn it, and act it out, it will set you free—even if your dad never changes at all.

15

Hold Me, Lord

A few minutes ago I hugged my eight-year-old, kissed him, and saw him go through the large, cold, steel doors of a large city hospital. Then I sat in the waiting room, 150 miles from home, considering what was most important in life.

Earlier, as I waited by Brandon's bed to meet the anesthesiologist, I felt that a friendly face was infinitely more valuable to us than fancy clothes, wealth, or the position of authority this doctor might hold. A hospital is a cold, scary place to start with, and Brandon was about to undergo the risk of a major, delicate operation rebuilding his inner ear.

Sitting in the waiting room for four hours, I realized how much more important people are than things. I prayed for God to please get Brandon through this, his third surgery in less than a year. I asked my heavenly Father to help the surgeon know exactly what to do, to give him the grace and dexterity to perform this delicate procedure correctly.

Around me, many people joked, laughed, and talked loudly. One group sang "Happy Birthday" to a woman. Twenty nearby conversations pounded into my brain. "How can they be acting so natural?" I wondered.

In my restlessness, I pictured all the things that could go wrong: A nerve could be severed, and Brandon's face would become paralyzed, or he could die from the anesthesia. All the things I'd been trying to avoid thinking about crashed in on me. I felt tired; I'd slept very little last night, worrying about my little boy.

When I read my devotional yesterday, it said that God allows disappointments and troubles in our lives to bring us closer to him and that we should love God even when things go wrong in our lives. Did God have me read that so I would understand why this operation went wrong?

I felt so scared that I could have cried if my mom had been there.

"I'm supposed to be strong for others, not scared and confused," I thought. "O Lord, I need you now, please hold me and help me. Give me peace," I prayed.

Then I remembered some words from Rich Mullins's song "Hold Me, Jesus":

> Hold me, Jesus,
> I'm shaking like a leaf.
> You have been my King of Glory,
> won't you be my Prince of Peace?

Maybe I'm not always the strong one for others, but God is always my strength.

> God is our refuge and strength,
> A very present help in trouble.
> Therefore we will not fear, though the earth should
>   change,
> And though the mountains slip into the heart of the
>   sea.
>
> Psalm 46:1–2

Are you tied in to the Prince of Peace, or are you still quaking in the waiting room?

16
Freed for Forgiveness

Recently I got a letter from a new Christian who was confused about something a friend had told her.

Dear Bill,
    A friend of mine, a strong Christian, tells me she gets strength from the fact that she has been forgiven of her sins. I'm not sure what she means. Can you help?
                                  Wondering

Though I can't be certain just what Wondering's friend said, I think she's communicating her own excitement at the wonderful feeling she has knowing that she is clean in God's sight. Rich in grace and God's love, she may be experiencing "the praise of the glory of His grace, which He freely bestowed on us in the Beloved" (Eph. 1:6).

Perhaps she knows what it means to be rescued from the hold Satan had on her: "For He delivered us from the domain of darkness, and transferred us to the kingdom of His beloved Son" (Col. 1:13).

Set a prisoner free from jail, and she will feel exhilarated, liberated, and strong. When we turn to Jesus and he forgives us, we may experience the same thing. We were meant to be free—and stay free—in God: "It was for freedom that Christ set us free; therefore keep standing firm and do not be subject again to a yoke of slavery" (Gal. 5:1).

Do you look forward to Christ's return and the thought of spending eternity with him? Are you "looking for the blessed hope and the appearing of the glory of our great God and Savior, Christ Jesus" (Tit. 2:13)? Does that cause you to get excited and make you want to serve him?

God has given us such abundant grace and forgiveness that picturing millions in hell for eternity should inspire us and give us strength to make every effort to save people from being forever separated from God. Why not help your friends and family experience the love God has for them, instead of an eternity full of regrets?

17
Taken for Granted

About eighty days a year I'm speaking to high-school students, addressing major conventions, or giving keynote speeches for businesses. I'm away from home a lot.

When I'm on the road, I notice that a lot of things are easier to do. It's easier to be nice to strangers for a few minutes or an hour than to be good to the loved ones who constantly live with me.

Most of us experience this at one time or another. Why? I believe it's because we're around our loved ones so much that we take them for granted. Sure, they know just how to tick us off. Your brother ate the last of the cereal. Your mom didn't iron your favorite outfit. Your sister scratched your bike or didn't clean out the extra-large order of fries from your car. Your dad lost your favorite tennis racket.

When things like that happen, it's easy to take people for granted.

But if one of your loved ones died suddenly, you'd give anything to have that person back. If you left the house angry because you'd fought with your mom and then she was killed in an accident, you'd regret it for the rest of your life. You see, you'd taken her for granted and never had a chance to say "I'm sorry."

For me, the biggest reason I'm not as nice at home as I am on the road is that in my house I expect to be served and waited on. I'm also much more preoccupied at home. It's hard for me to fit in a daily quiet time with God, which means I'm taking him for granted too. When I ignore the most important person in my life, it is easy to take for granted all the others I love as well.

I'm especially susceptible to taking God for granted in the summer when my kids are home and there's lots to do. We get up early and go outside to play all day. We have campfires at night. We have a great time together, but before you know it, it's the next day and I've had no time for God.

When I'm on the road, with no one asking me to jump rope, ride bikes, throw the ball, or talk with them, it's easy to spend hours with God. But I hate the fact that he has first place when I'm away from my family and has no place in my life when I'm home. I'm trying to change that.

I hope you carve out some time for yourself and God—don't take him for granted. Never let a busy schedule rob you of time for fellowship with your Creator.

When you are wise enough to recognize that people are more important than things, your family and Creator will always come first. Then you can avoid a home where alcoholism, abuse, wrong priorities, rage, or codependency take control.

If you are fortunate enough to have a mom, dad, brothers, and sisters, don't take them for granted either. Should you feel tempted to do that, visit someone who is alone or someone who lives with the shame and regret of forgetting to say "I love you" or "I'm sorry" before a family member left, never to come back.

When you are wise enough to recognize that people are more important than things, your family and Creator will always come first. Then you can avoid a home where alcoholism, abuse, wrong priorities, rage, or codependency take control.

With God's help, start loving and appreciating your family.

Do it for the Lord and the good of those around you, and your own heart will be blessed.

18
Guns or Bibles?

"I have a gun in one hand and a Bible in the other," announced an extremely depressed woman who called in on a Christian radio talk show. This desperate woman needed help fast. First the host talked her out of using the gun to end her life. Then the people involved in the program got her help with her problems. Because people cared, that woman made it through her difficult time.

Lots of people face desperation and doubt. When they lack the love they need to carry on, they may feel drawn to suicide. Or drugs may seem like a glittering way to end their problems. Others turn to one boyfriend after another, seeking the "comfort" of premarital sex.

Satan's methods of getting us into his clutches and keeping a hold on us look so good on the outside. But he doesn't let us see that behind the sparkle of sin lies agony. The hooting and hollering boozer on the corner may not be having fun at all. A promiscuous teen may learn the hard way that sex can bring pain, when she's raped by two friends of her boyfriend while he stands by watching.

Sin is ugly and painful, not something to laugh at. Satan doesn't care how our lives are ripped apart as long as he can nudge us down the wide, heavily trodden path of sin. While we're on that road, it's nearly impossible for us to see the straight, narrow path of Jesus. God's peace cannot be ours under those conditions. But he has provided the way of salvation, at the cost of his only Son's life.

That desperate woman held all the wisdom and love in the universe in one hand—and all the hatred of Satan in the other. It was up to her to make a choice between them. Her choice was to accept the Word and its Creator—Jesus.

Anyone who believes and trusts in Jesus discovers the truth penned by John: "Through him all things were made; without him nothing was made that has been made. In him was life, and that life was the light of men. The light shines in the darkness, but the darkness has not understood it" (John 1:3–5 NIV).

Today Jesus exposes darkness—the darkness that causes people to turn away from him and turn to guns or violence. Why do so many crimes occur at night? Because that's when people think they won't be seen. Most people get drunk and commit adultery at night because Satan is the ruler of the dark.

Now is the time to turn from the dark and into God's light. Turn away from the things that are wrong. Put down your gun and pick up his Word. Trust in him, and you will experience his love.

19

Gypped!

"This isn't worth it. I've been had!" Haven't you said those words when you bought something and then found out it wasn't worth the price?

The other day it happened to my son and daughter. They took the prize out of a cereal box that showed a bright yellow, illuminated saucer on the back of the carton. Two children were throwing one saucer, which looked almost motorized, shedding a six-foot trail of light behind it.

When my daughter unearthed the toy from the bottom of the box, hooked in the handle, and flicked her wrist to toss it, it fell to the floor. We tried again, and the thing shot in the wrong direction, almost taking off my wife's head. The third time it went end over end, like a knuckle ball.

"I've been had. What a gyp!" exclaimed Crystal as she held it up to the picture on the box. Of course, we only paid $2.38 for that cereal, and the prize was worth $.06, tops. So it wasn't any big deal.

But cereal-box toys aren't the only things that gyp you. Mistakes in your life can be much more costly. Paying with life-long regrets and a distorted personality or with a damaged reputation isn't worth the pain.

Recently Ted told me about the price he paid to drink and drive. Today he's a paraplegic because he went to a party and drove home drunk. "I can't miss this one," he'd thought, "I'm a party animal!" He had the reputation of finding the biggest bashes and putting away more booze than anyone else.

"I hated this image," Ted admitted. "I wish I could have stopped. The only good thing that's come out of my having to ride a wheelchair and losing half my back and the use of both legs is that I don't have to live up to that anymore.

"I paid too heavy a price. I wish I had listened to my friends and family. I wish I had stopped drinking and obeyed the law."

Since his accident, Ted has met the Lord. But even though God has given him a new heart, the sin scars from his bad decisions will stay with him throughout his life.

Sometimes you can take a risk, try something new, and step out of your comfort zone without getting hurt. Those are wise choices. But wrong decisions can harm you for a long time.

Every day of your life you can make wiser choices by spending a few moments thinking about the price for your activities. Will it be worth it to pay for years with a sexually transmitted disease for the pleasure of that one-night stand? Will separation from God—for a day, a week, or years—be worth a quick choice to take what you want, even though you can't afford those new jeans? Will the thrill of driving your dad's car be worth getting in trouble with the law and the family tension it causes?

Decide that it's not worth it! The price is too high.

Before buying an expensive appliance for their home, intelligent shoppers look in *Consumers Digest* to discover the best buys. When it comes to decision making, the Holy Bible helps you make the best purchase for your life. "From Thy precepts I get understanding; therefore I hate every false way" (Ps. 119:104).

Get the best value for your soul and life by turning away from wrong. You know what to do. The Bible gave you the directions.

20
Happy Tears

"Happy birthday to you . . ." I heard the song from the kitchen area of the local restaurant while I was sitting there writing. My waitress came out to wait on tables, and several groups of her regular customers began singing "Happy Birthday" to her too. As she hugged one woman, I heard the customer say, "Those are happy tears. You go right ahead and cry."

Happy tears are indeed a blessing. Everyone deserves times when others pay attention to them, sing to them, hug them, and encourage them to cry happy tears. But not everyone is fortunate enough to get that.

Betty, the birthday girl, had received that recognition because over the years of serving others she handed out thousands of smiles, thousands of cups of coffee, and courtesy and politeness as a way of life, even though she got mashed potatoes and gravy spilled down the front of her apron more times than she could count. Though her feet were aching, she remained one of the nicest people I know.

Put that kind of love into action, and you will be appreciated too. Each of us can look for a need and fill it with a smile. Today you could

- do something that will lighten your mom's load.
- find a girl at school who is left out by the in-crowd and offer your friendship.

- thank your teacher for taking the extra time to make the subject interesting.
- give your all at your job with a cheerful spirit.
- stay polite even when the lunch you are rushing to the rude, impatient customer spills to the floor.

Do you smile, even when it hurts? If so, people will love to be around you. Throughout your life, you will receive lots of hugs and will find lots of reasons to cry happy tears.

Betty is a picture of the verse that says: "Offer hospitality to one another without grumbling. Each one should use whatever gift he has received to serve others, faithfully administering God's grace in its various forms" (1 Peter 4:9–10 NIV). So don't grumble, or it will spoil your serve.

21
Hard or Soft?

Female rappers with vulgar mouths top the pop charts with their profanity and rough and tough images. Why? It sells!

USA Today quoted public-relations people from various record labels, who reported, "Nobody wants to be perceived as soft, not even females." "The market dictates their direction." And, "The girls had to go that way—be tough, strong and 'street'—the kids want to hear it."

"Some entertainers will do anything for money," you might say. But what about you and me? Do we like being thought of as soft? Do you want to be called pure, honest, and kind, or must you fit in with the world at all costs?

Can you be the real you, or are you too busy measuring up to what others might think to let people know the truth? Have you become an entertainer, who tries to win friendship and admiration by changing colors like a chameleon?

The toughest part of being a professional entertainer who is after ratings, cash, and popularity is that the world, not God, dictates who you are. But you don't have to be a professional entertainer to let the world tell you what to do. It's the same for people who fear that someone will disapprove of them, so they try to please the crowd instead of listening to God.

Are you looking up or out for approval? If you are looking up to God, you could find that being soft and saved isn't so bad after all!

Do you want to be called pure, honest, and kind, or must you fit in with the world at all costs?

God is the ultimate critic, and he has a terrific reward that's worth more than everything in this earth.

22

No Second-Best Heroes

Her beautiful smile can light up a room. But at eleven years old, Lisa has a rare disease that makes her bones very brittle. When she walks the halls in her school, she has to be careful. A fall could break her leg. If someone bumps into her, she could crack a rib.

The doctors don't have any answers. But when I met Lisa and her mother after my speech, I was taken aback by this brave girl's face. Brilliant love, joy, and beauty radiated from her eyes.

As we talked, Lisa told me about a paper she had just written about heroes. "I want you to know that my hero is God, and I was proud to tell my entire class about him," she shared. "I'll never be ashamed of him."

Though she has every reason to be angry at God—since she has an incurable physical problem that may shorten her life—Lisa loves God and is proud of him. She gives him the thanks and praise he deserves. Lisa isn't looking for a pity party. She's excited about life and the Giver of life, who is her hero.

We need this kind of better model for heroes today. We've glorified the superstar in prison or dying of AIDS. We've looked up to the musician who uses any lyric or tactic to rake in the bucks. But we need something better to base our lives on.

I hope God is on your list of heroes. His love and patience should show you how much he loves you. Mold your life on his gentleness, kindness, and courage to stand for a cause.

Find other heroes too—men and women who can help you live as a strong Christian. Some of the best heroes don't get their names in lights or on billboards. They may sit quietly in the corners of your life, until you are ready to notice them. They aren't looking for their own glory, so maybe you pass them by. Your mom cleans your house day in and day out so you can live in a comfortable environment. Your dad may pray for you every day. Your grandma may help people in the community without expecting anything in return.

When you look for heroes, don't focus on popularity. Choose someone who has good qualities on the inside, whom you can look up to and model your life after. Approachable, down-to-earth people make the best models. Don't seek out someone who can't admit to making mistakes. Everyone needs to be able to say, "I goofed. I need God too."

Pick a famous person as your hero, and you won't have someone nearby who can take time to help you, pray for you, and support you. Look up to someone who has done unbelievable things because she has many gifts from God, but not if all she has to offer are her abilities. Choose someone who has accomplished much and spreads goodness, someone who will not tolerate lack of character.

Choose the right hero—and become a hero to someone else in the process. No second-best heroes need apply!

23
Knowing His Will

On a plane trip from Memphis to Detroit, I was writing out a prayer when the flight attendant noticed my Bible. She shared with me that she felt concerned that she might never know God's will. "I wonder who will be 'Mr. Right' for me," she admitted. "Life isn't supposed to be easy, and we may never know God's will for our lives," she went on.

As she talked, it became obvious that she expected more bad things to happen to her than good ones—her outlook was anything but hopeful. So I shared two ways I have trusted to know God's will in my life.

"First," I shared, "if you are saved and in the Word daily, striving to be like Jesus in all you do—follow the desires of your heart." I showed her Matthew 7:7, "Ask, and it shall be given to you; seek, and you shall find; knock, and it shall be opened to you." I told her, "Your will aligns with God's will if you live for him this way."

As a second step, I encouraged her to walk with God day by day, striving to be free of sin. "Sin blocks you from hearing God's voice," I warned. Then I showed her these passages from Proverbs 1:24–26, 28:

> Because I called, and you refused;
> I stretched out my hand, and no one paid attention;
> And you neglected all my counsel,

And did not want my reproof;
I will even laugh at your calamity;
I will mock when your dread comes, . . .
Then they will call on me, but I will not answer;
They will seek me diligently, but they shall not find
    me.

When you sin, you are no longer in total fellowship with God. Your desires are no longer his desires, and that's not God's plan for you: "This I say therefore, and affirm together with the Lord, that you walk no longer just as the Gentiles also walk, in the futility of their mind" (Eph. 4:17).

Before you make a decision, ask yourself, "What would Jesus do?" By following in his footsteps, you will develop a life that pleases him. Strive to be sin free, and your outlook will become positive and hopeful.

God doesn't want to hide his will from you. That's why he gave you his Book, revealing who he is and what he wants for your life. Get into it and learn about his will. You can be sure that God isn't trying to lead you into trouble, make life difficult, or cause you to doubt his love. He's not giving the hardest test with trick questions just to make you squirm.

When you run into that sort of thing, look around, because it may be Satan who's at your side. That's a will you won't want to get involved with.

24
Masked!

Yvonne was an all-round student who excelled in sports, had perfect looks, attracted lots of friends, made good grades, and was liked by all her teachers.

Would you like to be in her shoes? Yvonne wouldn't.

"I guess you'd say I'm insecure," she confessed. "I'm afraid to be myself. It's as if a mask covers what I'm really like. When I'm with one of my friends at practice, I laugh at her jokes, even if I don't think they're funny. Whatever she wants to do, I just go along with it. I'm different when I'm studying with another friend. But I go along with her too."

The eighteen-year-old lamented, "I don't know who I am anymore. Seems as if I'm always pleasing others. I lack confidence and a mind of my own. I'm tired of being like a dumb sparrow, following the flock with my mask on."

I counseled Yvonne, "Whenever you try to please others, you will fall short. No matter what you do, you can never please everyone. So don't waste your life trying to do it.

"People who really care for you don't want you to be anyone but yourself anyway," I encouraged her. "Masks are really a waste of time because they lead you into never-never land. You will never, never like yourself if you play the please-others-to-fit-in game."

Yvonne needed to accept herself completely, and I showed her how that could happen.

Do you feel as if you know what Yvonne's talking about because you've been walking in her shoes lately? If so, you can use the following guidelines for accepting yourself:

Begin by accepting your Maker and Designer. I challenge you to totally accept Jesus as your Lord and Savior. Until you put your total trust in him for your life and salvation, you'll never be freed from your sins and feel reborn. He has created each of us to be unique and wonderful. To discover your own real self, read his Word.

"The law of Thy mouth is better to me than thousands of gold and silver pieces. Thy hands made me and fashioned me; give me understanding, that I may learn Thy commandments" (Ps. 119:72–73).

Trust in the One who has a plan for your life and follow in his pathway. "Teach me Thy way, O LORD; I will walk in Thy truth; unite my heart to fear Thy name" (Ps. 86:11). As you trust in God, not people, he will never let you down. The psalmist could say, "I wait for the LORD, my soul does wait, and in His word do I hope" (Ps. 130:5), because he had read God's promises and knew God would keep them.

Act like the real you, knowing that God is standing by your side. "Do not rejoice over me, O my enemy; though I fall I will rise; though I dwell in darkness, the LORD is a light for me" (Mic. 7:8). "His [a righteous man's] heart is upheld, he will not fear, until he looks with satisfaction on his adversaries" (Ps. 112:8).

God does not wear a mask, and he wants to know the real you even more than you want to know him. "Glory in His holy name; let the heart of those who seek the LORD be glad" (Ps. 105:3).

You may think people will like you more for being what they want you to be. In fact, no one will hate you for being yourself; they will admire you. God wants you to stand up for who you are and what you believe in. "Be on the alert, stand firm in the faith, act like men, be strong" (1 Cor. 16:13). "Because he has loved Me, therefore I will deliver him; I will set him securely on high, because he has known My name" (Ps. 91:14).

When you pretend to be something you are not, you lie to the world. "Do not lie to one another, since you laid aside the old self with its evil practices" (Col. 3:9). Show others the real you because when you are with Jesus you have nothing to hide.

Take off your mask, get real, and have a laugh with your friend in the mirror. You may really be meeting her for the first time.

25
Minor Miracles

You may be the only Jesus some people see. A song on the radio reminded me of that, and I know how true it is. Our hands help unfortunate people. Our feet lead the hurting. Our mouths speak the truth about God and life.

But imagine if we refused to take action. How would people know that God was real? How would they hear of the great things he's done?

Imitate God with your actions because through you he is reaching the world. "Therefore be imitators of God, as beloved children; and walk in love, just as Christ also loved you" (Eph. 5:1–2).

"I can't imitate God. Only God can work miracles," you may object. "I could never give sight to the blind or speech to the dumb. I can't make someone hear if they are deaf. Obviously I could never bring a dead person back to life."

But I think you can work minor miracles every day. People you come in contact with at home or school may live as if they were dead. They may have no hope, be depressed, and feel as if they've been beaten down, run over. The world seems to be against them. Give them light to see by, encouragement to keep them going, and a hug when they need it. Send a note in the mail. Bring your mom breakfast in bed. Say, "I'll clean my room today," or, "Let me mow the lawn."

Little things like that give light to people and bring them back from the dark corners of depression. You may pull someone off the cliff of emotional death by showing you care.

Put your arm around a depressed friend's shoulders and say, "You are very special in God's eyes." Encourage the girl who's just been cut from the team by inviting her over. Ask someone who hasn't had a date in several months, "Want to sit with us at the game this weekend?"

When I was in high school, hearing those words from the right people could have saved my life. They would have kept me from doing so many foolish things in college in an attempt to feel important.

My kids are only in elementary school, but already they need to feel included. When a friend talks about them behind their backs, they get bummed. When they trip in front of someone, and that person starts to laugh, they come home crying.

No matter how old you are, some things will get you down. At forty-four, with fourteen books to my name, I still get depressed if I fall in front of someone and that person laughs. But the encouragement of a friend can pick me up right away.

Make miracles by giving sight to the student who can't see that if she keeps on drinking, she could become an alcoholic. Show her the truth, and let God rid her of her blind spot.

As long as you avoid sharing, you can't give her sight. Your fear of anger and rejection might be real. But as a wise person told me: If someone can't see, and you have the glasses that would suit her perfectly but don't offer them, you are the blind person.

Don't blow the opportunities God puts before you. Recently I heard a friend say he passed up the opportunity to tell an unsaved friend about Jesus. Last week that man died, and my friend will always feel the pain of knowing that he could have shared Jesus—and didn't.

Make the deaf hear by being the voice that tells a friend the words she can't hear from her parents. Those words may be:

"Premarital sex is wrong."

"Don't cheat, it won't be to your advantage in the long run."

"Lying will only ruin your relationship with your parents."

You may have seen your friend turn away from the truth, scoffing at those who told her. She's deaf. But when you don't speak up, you're dumb. Don't lose one-time opportunities to make someone listen and to let her know you care. Make her hear, even though her ears have been shut for so long.

Give utterance to those who have never told their parents they love them. Maybe your dad has never said it to his dad. Or maybe for years you haven't heard those words from your mom.

"Well," a friend may object, "I don't hug because my dad doesn't hug. His parents never hugged him because theirs never hugged them. They're from the old country. That's just the way we do things."

Guess what. That's the way things used to be around here, but you can change them. Start by speaking the truth and getting others to do it too. Say something, and you can start to believe it. Feel it as God builds the dream in your mind. With his love and encouragement, it can reach your heart.

Even when you don't have the right words, share anyway. Many people won't go into a hospital or to a funeral home because they don't have the right words. They feel dumb and can't speak. Guess what—hardly anyone has the right words for such situations. But just being there shouts "I love you" loud and clear. A simple card in the mail announces "I care" as if you'd held up a megaphone to your lips and spoken the words. Calling, even when your friend won't return your calls, says "I need you, even though I am too proud to admit it."

Work a miracle for the dead, deaf, dumb, or blind today. Look around for those people. You may be the only Jesus they can see, hear, or respond to.

26
So Far yet So Near

Traveling by car, train, or plane, I can still stay close to my friends and family. Whether I'm in the States or abroad, they are never more than a few feet away. Even David Copperfield, the magician, can't duplicate this "trick of the trade" that really isn't a trick and doesn't have a trade.

When I was a little boy I first heard of this amazing activity. People told me how wonderful it was and that my parents would think highly of me if I did it every day. The problem was, it was so boring that I didn't make it part of my life. Besides, everyone who told me about it never did it, to my knowledge, so I figured they were lying.

Several years ago I met the inventor of this amazing activity, and I found that it can keep your family close and help you unleash the most awesome powers in the universe. The more I trusted the inventor of this phenomenon and used his method, the better it worked.

"What kind of modern-day voodoo is this?" you may wonder.

It isn't voodoo of any kind. It's prayer, and this is how I've found it works:

> If a list of people you are praying for,
> is looked at every day;

and poured over with your pleadings,
they will never be far away.

The apostle Paul knew the power of prayer to keep Christians close. That's why he wrote:

We give thanks to God always for all of you, making mention of you in our prayers.

1 Thessalonians 1:2

For what thanks can we render to God for you in return for all the joy with which we rejoice before our God on your account, as we night and day keep praying most earnestly that we may see your face, and may complete what is lacking in your faith? Now may our God and Father Himself and Jesus our Lord direct our way to you; and may the Lord cause you to increase and abound in love for one another, and for all men, just as we also do for you.

1 Thessalonians 3:9–12

You will never forget something that's important to your loved ones if you pray for them each day. When you travel, always remember to pack a quiet-time book with a list of your prayer needs and the needs of others. Day by day, take each one to the throne of God. "Let my cry come near before Thee, O LORD; give me understanding according to Thy word" (Ps. 119:169). If you are in right standing with him, God will hear your pleadings.

Your loved ones are only a prayer away. That's because the inventor of prayer has promised he will never be anywhere but by your side. Go to him often, and even when you are gone, your heart will still be at home.

27
Party Perspective

Before a Friday evening program I gave in Saint Mary's, Ohio, five girls came over to me. Their leader said, "We all came from my Sweet Sixteen party to hear you."

"You gave up your party to hear me speak on ways to better your family?" I asked, amazed. "I'm impressed, and I sure do appreciate it!" When I asked why they came, they explained that the daytime program I'd given to the students had touched them, and they wanted to learn more.

Those teens are rare people because they had a deep desire to learn, grow, and gain wisdom. Though they may not have realized it, they were following in Jesus' footsteps.

Our Lord loved to learn and ask questions, as his parents discovered when they took him to Jerusalem for the first time. When it was time to go home, they had to form a search party. No one had seen Jesus! "And it came about that after three days they found Him in the temple, sitting in the midst of the teachers, both listening to them, and asking them questions" (Luke 2:46). During his teen years, the verse that best describes him is: "And Jesus kept increasing in wisdom and stature, and in favor with God and men" (Luke 2:52).

If you want to become great in God's eyes, you'll spend time learning how to please him. Moses was that kind of person. He asked God, "Now therefore, I pray Thee, if I have found favor in Thy sight, let me know Thy ways, that I may know Thee, so that I may find favor in Thy sight. Consider too, that this nation is Thy people" (Exod. 33:13).

People are living things, and like other living things, they either grow or die. Start growing today by learning something new from the Scriptures. Take your questions and cares to God.

Those girls will always impress me because teens who seek wisdom over pleasure are rare creatures indeed.

28
Perfection Expectations

After writing fourteen books and traveling all over the world to help kids and their parents, I expected my family to be problem free.

Wrong!

To remedy the situation, I took action. I tried harder, went to a counselor, read more books, and wrote more books. I got counseling for my family and tried harder again. But I still wasn't getting ahead.

Why didn't things change? Because my expectations of perfection never stopped. I spent time fighting and arguing with my family over the imperfections instead of enjoying Holly and my kids and growing with them.

The danger of expecting perfection is that it never happens. You don't get excitement and thrills in life every day. Sometimes the down days, filled with boredom, can't be avoided. Life simply won't meet you on your own terms.

What does it take to change perfectionism into realism? The secret is to overcome negative, demanding thinking so that we can enjoy ourselves, the people around us, God, and life.

Enjoy each moment for what it is. Live as if each and every moment might be your last, as if you'll never get it back again. Know that you can live for the moment because "we know that God causes all things to work together for good to those who love God, to those who are called according to His purpose" (Rom. 8:28).

Enjoy each moment for what it is. Live as if each and every moment might be your last, as if you'll never get it back again.

If trials come, enjoy the opportunity to put your faith to the test. When your little brother tries to upset you, make the most of this opportunity and take control of your mind, thoughts, and actions, and forgive him. If your mom asks you to do more than your sister, take advantage of this character-building process.

Most of the things you worry about never come to pass, but they can damage your relationship with God. When you start to worry and become demanding, your faith and thoughts toward God can quickly become negative and destructive.

Instead of letting a "might be" damage your spiritual life, fight back by reading Psalms or Proverbs. Study the life of David or Paul.

Life won't be a bed of roses. It hasn't been that way for anyone else, and it won't be so for you or me. Even though he was God's Son, Jesus didn't expect a perfect life in which everyone waited on him. Instead, he served his own disciples, doing even the most menial task:

> Jesus, knowing that the Father had given all things into His hands, and that He had come forth from God, and was going back to God, rose from supper, and laid aside His garments; and taking a towel, He girded Himself about. Then He poured water into the basin, and began

to wash the disciples' feet, and to wipe them with the towel with which he was girded.

John 13:3–5

Jesus knew where he came from and why he was serving, so even the most debasing task became an act of love. He didn't have to worry about what other people would think when he knelt to scrub the dirt off his disciples' toes.

We, too, can draw strength from knowing the reasons behind our actions. That can keep us on course, even when the troubles strike. When circumstances, people, and negative thoughts would control our attitudes and actions, we can turn them aside and take control of all we think, say, or do.

Still having trouble overcoming those perfection expectations? Take a close look at the things that influence your thought life. If you aren't pleased with the thoughts and actions coming out of your life—and you know God isn't either—realize that what you do is influenced by what you're thinking, and what you think is a result of what you read and listen to.

Whatever you put into your mind will come out in the form of thoughts, words, and actions. So before you listen to those lyrics, sit down to watch a movie, or pick a life-motivating philosophy, decide if it comes from the world or from God. Put more of God's nourishment in your mind by Scripture reading, going to church, and fellowshipping with those who love him, and your thoughts and actions will make a turnaround.

Look around you. Life is waiting for your contribution, not your critique. Don't wait for others to please you; instead build a better day by pleasing your Master.

Enjoy!

29

A Great Way to Pray

"Don't tell me I have to pray; it's just too hard. Why, I fall asleep whenever I try it!"

Like Nancy, who spoke these words, you may have found praying hard work. Maybe you've been looking at prayer as a miserable part of being a Christian, so you avoid it as much as possible.

If so, you've missed the point. Praying is actually a chance to talk to God—the Creator of the universe. It's not an optional part of the Christian life but a vital element of spiritual growth because it keeps you in touch with God.

Look in the Gospels and you will see that Jesus often spent time alone with God in prayer. In the midst of a busy ministry, "He Himself would often slip away to the wilderness and pray" (Luke 5:16). If God's Son needed to communicate with the Father, how much more we need to keep in touch!

If the knowledge that you are talking with the Creator won't keep you awake, I have a prayer method that will. You'll still have to set aside a few minutes each day to spend with God, but using a journal will help you remember what he has done for you and focus your attention.

Morning is by far the best time to pray because you can reflect on what God tells you and it can influence your entire day. Begin by spending time in the Bible. Then just talk to God and write it down. Fill a page a day. Tell God how wonderful he is. (If you are reading the Psalms, you will get lots of great ideas for this.) Tell him what you did the day before and how you goofed up, and ask him to help you stay away from that sin today. Record the things he has done to help you too.

By writing out your prayers as if you were writing a letter to a friend, you will become closer to him. All through the day you'll be able to remember what you asked for and how God responded. You'll also be making a record that you can look back on when Satan tempts you to doubt God. Record the things God has done for you, and you will prove that he answers prayers.

For years I've been writing out my prayers, and I've found that when I set aside a quiet place in the morning, the day goes more smoothly. Disastrous days often happened when I did not spend that time with God.

Stay close to your Creator, Savior, and best friend by keeping in touch. Start your journal today!

30
Enjoy the Real Life

How would you live if you knew that no sin could overtake you today? Well, you can do it, if you are willing to trust in God. That's what Paul was talking about when he wrote: "I have been crucified with Christ: and I myself no longer live, but Christ lives in me. And the real life I now have within this body is a result of my trusting in the Son of God, who loves me and gave himself for me" (Gal. 2:20 TLB).

No matter what sin Satan throws at you today, whether it's cheating on your chemistry test or spreading a damaging rumor, you have the power to say no. Being crucified with Jesus means that your old sin nature died just as Jesus died for you on the cross. Because it is dead, that old nature can't control you anymore. Jesus rose from the dead to give you his resurrection power. Christ now lives in you, and if you allow him to, he will also live through you, enabling you to say no to sin.

Today let your actions be his actions. Before you do something, ask if he would do that. Don't say anything he wouldn't say or do what you would feel ashamed to do if he were standing right beside you. Think before you speak and act.

The real life that is in your body is your life in Jesus. Let it come out all day as you release his power into the world. Ever since you trusted Jesus for your salvation and eternal life, he has been in you. He wants you to take on his likeness.

Let others see you act like Jesus. Let your family notice that you sound different, that you have higher standards and more gentle words. Let your friends see that you aren't too good to help someone, no matter what his or her position or popularity. Treat people with respect. As they watch, they may start to wish they were more like you because your actions reflect what you think and believe.

Knowing that Jesus loved you enough to die for you should give you the strength to keep your mind on the real life that Jesus gave you. Let that life shine for the whole world to see today.

31

Living in the Real World

"These are the nineties! What right do you have to impose your beliefs on others?" The topic was "Right and Wrong," and I had struck a nerve with the national talk-show host, who responded by trying to make me look bad.

"People who encourage teens to abstain from sex have forgotten what strong urges the sex drive brings to the scene. Who gave you the right to impose your views on others?" she repeated.

I'd agreed to go on the show because I thought it would be good publicity for my books. Though I realized the publicity had just turned sour, I tried to continue with my message. But every time I tried to talk about moral absolutes, she kept interrupting me, insisting, "No teen in America would listen to you!"

You could say we had different agendas, right from the start.

"I'm twenty-two now, and I'm much more mature because of the things I have done," a caller agreed with my host's stand. "I know myself a lot better because I've had sex, partied, and used drugs. I've lived through it, and so have my friends!" he boasted. "Besides, I might not get married for ten years. I suppose you expect me to stay away from sex all that time!" Disbelief filled his voice.

He probably thought I was from Mars. "Wake up to the real world!" he ended.

Yes, I agree that we all need to wake up to the real world. But right and wrong are the real world!

What are you willing to do for something you know is right? Do you stand for some absolutes? I mean, do you really believe in them to the point where you would lose your friendship with everyone in your school before you'd break this promise to yourself?

Whether or not you realize it, you have some core ideals—things you really believe in, promises you've made to yourself. Strong principles like this may be broken, but they don't change if you really believe in them. If you break them once in a while, it hurts, and you purpose to stick to them better the next time. Anything you own this way tells the world a lot about you.

What you believe in down deep may surprise you. For example, you may say that you don't believe in premarital sex, but when someone looks you straight in the eye and says that having sex before or outside of marriage is wrong, what do you do?

If you're normal, you probably get a little angry. The words "This guy thinks he's a know-it-all" probably flash through your mind. As your thoughts slip into gear at about 190 words a minute, your defense starts.

"What gives you the right to tell me what's right and wrong? You're not perfect!

"I'll do what I want, and nobody is going to be Mr. Righteous to me. You've had your head in the sand, Mr. Positive Man; and it's clear to everyone but you that you think the rest of us should live in a convent and be happy praying and fasting all day long, like you."

Sound familiar? Maybe the words condemning premarital sex made the hairs on the back of your neck stand up. If so, you're not unusual. Like me, and millions of others on Planet Earth, you don't like to be told what to do. Still, that doesn't mean you can't recognize right when you hear it.

Okay, I should have responded more gently and tactfully to the talk-show host. It could have helped the message reach a lot more people. Despite my mistake, a few others did hear my message. A mother called in and chewed out the host for cutting me down. "He's giving the advice I and many of my friends needed to hear," she commented.

Maybe I'm not always the most tactful adviser. I can't claim that I always get the words right. But if you're really looking for it, you can hear the truth—no matter who tells you. Because the truth always come from God, no matter what the messenger looks like.

When it comes to doing right, what has the last say? Will popularity, fear of disagreeing with your parents, or the attitudes of the rest of the world influence you at the moment you stand up to be counted? Does your mind, heart, feelings, or God's Word end the discussion when you weigh right and wrong?

The truth you're looking for is in the Bible, which can separate what's real and lasting from what's only going to feel good in the short term. If you've never read the Scriptures to find out about the real world, pick up a Bible today. Learn about the path God has blazed for you, and you can feel his touch on your life and desire to follow in his way.

Once you've been touched by God and want his wisdom, you have a lot to offer the world. As you learn from him, you'll be able to help others look in the Book for their answers to life's questions.

Nothing is perfect except your words. Oh, how I love them. I think about them all day long. They make me wiser than my enemies, because they are my constant guide. Yes, wiser than my teachers, for I am ever thinking of your rules. They make me even wiser than the aged.

I have refused to walk the paths of evil for I will remain obedient to your Word.

No, I haven't turned away from what you taught me; your words are sweeter than honey. And since only your rules can give me wisdom and understanding, no wonder I hate every false teaching.

Psalm 119:96–104 TLB

Once the talk show finished, I did what we all do so well—I replayed the scene over and over in my mind. "My host didn't like me," I told myself. "If I'd just said this. . . ," and I imagined myself speaking words that would have made her like me. "Maybe saying that would have increased my popularity on the talk-show circuit," I thought.

That's when my Scripture study paid off. Right between my pride and my need to be loved by everyone, I was struck by a powerful verse from my favorite set of instructions:

You are like an unfaithful wife who loves her husband's enemies. Don't you realize that making friends with God's enemies—the evil pleasures of this world—makes you an enemy of God? I say it again, that if your aim is to enjoy the evil pleasure of the unsaved world, you cannot also be a friend of God.

James 4:4 TLB

Pretty strong stuff, huh? Do you think God is deterred from speaking the truth when we complain that we don't like his strong words? He's not fazed by our opinion—he only speaks what's right, not what people want to hear.

Then I thought of the fellow who called in and seemed to think I was from Mars. God explained that situation to me through another verse: "Satan, who is the god of this evil world, has made him [the one on the road to eternal death] blind, unable to see the glorious light of the Gospel that is shining upon him, or to understand the amazing message we preach about the glory of Christ, who is God" (2 Cor. 4:4 TLB).

Still, I hadn't gotten the message—it was as if I wanted to have my hot fudge sundae and not gain weight. I kept looking for a way out of stating the truth when others found it unpleasant. So God reminded me:

> Anyone who wants to be my follower must love me far more than he does his own father, mother, wife, children, brothers, or sisters—yes, more than his own life—otherwise he cannot be my disciple. And no one can be my disciple who does not carry his own cross and follow me.
>
> Luke 14:26–27 TLB

My cross is to tell the truth—whether on the radio or in the pages of this book. You bear the same cross if you know Jesus. When the world disagrees, we can remember what Jesus said to the talk-show hosts of his day:

> You search the Scriptures, for you believe they give you eternal life. And the Scriptures point to me! Yet you won't come to me so that I can give you this life eternal!
>
> Your approval or disapproval means nothing to me, for as I know so well, you don't have God's love within you. I know, because I have come to you representing my Father and you refuse to welcome me, though you readily enough receive those who aren't sent from him, but represent only themselves!
>
> John 5:39–43 TLB

Living in the real world doesn't mean that everyone thinks you're a nice person. It doesn't mean you go with the flow and never ruffle any feathers. Those who tell the truth will find people pointing fingers in their faces and crying out against them.

Eternal life's kind of costly, isn't it?

32

Refocused

During an interview, Larry King asked Jimmy Carter if television news programs could help end wars.

"They can help us focus on the suffering," the former president answered.

He's right. When you see starving people in a remote part of the world, bones protruding through their skin, flies all over their eyes, it may help you focus on their suffering instead of your own small problems. Throughout the day, you may have trouble getting their pain out of your mind.

President Carter's statement challenged me to refocus my thoughts on hurting people. "Sure," I thought, "I went to Russia to help people, but do I ignore the suffering in my own backyard, in my own church, or my own family? We sponsor a child through Compassion International and faithfully send our money in each month, but do I notice when my own kids hurt? Maybe I'm in such a rush to get in that extra golf game that I avoid spending time pushing the kids on the swing or just talking with them."

What am I focusing on? Do I just walk past the suffering that's nearby?

When my buddies and I go to play golf, we begin with a prayer that we will be good witnesses and please God. Often when I open my eyes after the prayer, it's so bright out that I see spots for a couple of hours. Because my head is spinning, it becomes impossibly hard for me to focus on the ball or have good balance.

In life, we can get spots before our eyes too. When I get busy wondering what other people think of me, I can't notice others. When I worry about what I'll say next, I can't remember people's names. I'm focusing on the spots, so I can't look at the really important things.

God's Word warns us not to be self-centered:

> Do nothing from selfishness or empty conceit, but with humility of mind let each of you regard one another as more important than himself; do not merely look out for your own personal interests, but also for the interests of others.
>
> Philippians 2:3–4

We're not meant to get so caught up in ourselves that we don't see the needs and suffering of others.

Don't eat all of your family's favorite cereal. Or if your sister leaves dirty clothes in the bathroom, don't say, "I didn't leave them there. Why should I pick them up?" Put them in the hamper for her. Remember that if your mom had the same attitude, your house would be crowded with items that were never put away.

Focus on the suffering of other people by serving them. Instead of asking, "What's in it for me?" help them as if you were helping Jesus himself. Then he will be able to say to you:

> I was hungry, and you gave Me something to eat; I was thirsty, and you gave Me drink; I was a stranger, and you invited Me in; naked, and you clothed Me; I was sick, and you visited Me; I was in prison, and you came to Me. . . .
>
> Truly I say to you, to the extent that you did it to one of these brothers of Mine, even the least of them, you did it to Me.
>
> Matthew 25:35–36, 40

Today, look around for someone who is hurting. Don't wait for a classmate to slit her wrists before you notice that she's sad. Don't avoid her because she's quieter, walking a little slower, and stays away from other people.

Suffering is all around you; you just need to open your eyes to see it. Refocus, and you can help Jesus solve the problems of your world.

33

Rules That Can't Be Broken

Did you know that there are some rules you can't break? You may be able to drive over the speed limit, drink and drive, or cross the street when the light is red. But not every law is that easy to ignore.

Get out of bed, put your feet down, lean forward, and you will stand upright instead of floating to the ceiling. Jump off a building, and you will hit the ground. The law of gravity always works. You can't break it, no matter what you do.

Well, there's a spiritual law that you can't break either, no matter how hard you try. It's stated in Romans 6:23: "The wages of sin is death."

Get a job, work hard, and you get a wage—a paycheck at the end of the week. In the same way, if you work hard at sinning, you will be paid—though the check isn't as pleasant. You see, those who never accept Christ suffer eternal separation from him. That's spiritual death.

Even Christians experience this truth. Something inside dies every time a Christian sins. A young woman wrote me to say that she didn't follow her heart and the truth taught by her parents. After having premarital sex, she found out that she has AIDS. Though she's accepted Christ and will go to heaven, she can't rid herself of the disease or change its ultimate course.

If young people rebel against their parents, even though they restore the relationship years later, they discover that something has died. A part of what was between them and their parents is gone. Life will never be the same, even if they come to an understanding with Mom and Dad.

Many years ago I wrote a letter to a friend. At the time, I was angry, and I said things that should never have been said. Today I understand that I should have written the letter, stamped and addressed it, and then torn it up and thrown it in the garbage. But because I didn't understand that when I wrote the letter, it killed the relationship.

Saying things in anger deals death. It may be the end of a friendship or of hope. Your words may destroy your future. Some kind of death will always follow sin.

In a Sunday school class, I once taught an object lesson that used a board, various nails, and a hammer. I asked the teens what types of sins we committed as kids.

"Lying, stealing, fighting, cussing," they answered. For each one I pounded a small nail in the board.

"What kinds of sins do we commit when we're a little older?" I questioned.

They named the same sins and added some more: "premarital sex, cheating, disobedience." I added some larger nails to the board.

"As adults, what kinds of sins are most regretted?" I wanted to know.

"Adultery, dishonesty, hypocrisy, unfaithfulness, abuse," they answered. I drove the largest nails in the wood.

"We've all sinned," I told them, showing them the board. "With Christ, our sins can be forgiven and wiped away." I started to pull out the nails, to show them what happens when we trust in Jesus.

"What do you see now?" I asked, after every nail was out.

"All kinds of holes, shattered wood, an unmendable surface," they responded.

"Of course, in God's eyes all those sins are gone," I shared. "But sometimes we have to live with the scars. It might be a disease or a limb that got chopped off. It might be the results of an accident that took place when you were driving under the influence. Though you've been forgiven, you still spend your life in that wheelchair."

The difference between good and evil, right and wrong, God and Satan, will never change. Don't listen when friends tell you that partying with the sinners is better than dying with the saints. Deep down, you know that's a lie.

Die to yourself and let the Lord come alive in your life. You can start overcoming death today!

34
Save the Day!

If you have a blowup with your mom, sister, or best friend, does it ruin your whole day? When I was a kid, it would have ruined that day—and maybe a few after it. You see, if we had a fight in my home, we stayed mad for several days.

But a bad experience doesn't have to ruin even one day. The first time I realized that, I'd just received rejection from a group of speakers. I felt depressed. But inside my heart, I knew God was bigger and stronger than this. With him I could bounce out of depression and make the most of the day before me. God gave me the key to changing the day: "Therefore, prepare your minds for action; be self-controlled" (1 Peter 1:13 NIV).

I knew I could take control of my own thoughts, by deciding what to think and hope on. Depression and worry didn't have to overtake me. By controlling my own thoughts, I could have God as my strength to regain a better mental balance.

Train yourself to bounce back from negative situations. Remember, a bad moment isn't a bad day—unless you turn it into one! Don't believe in the myths that today is a wreck because it's raining, because it's your least-favorite season, or because you have no date for Saturday night. "Have nothing to do with godless myths and old wives' tales; rather, train yourself to be godly" (1 Tim. 4:7 NIV).

Temptations, disagreements, and differences of opinion come and go. Everyone (even Jesus) has experienced trouble.

We can't control what the world throws at us, but we can decide how to respond to it. We can decide how long to stay in the dumps.

Don't expect good, peaceful feelings just to come over you, filling you with joy. You'll have to work for them. "So then, dear friends, since you are looking forward to this [the second coming of Jesus], make every effort to be found spotless, blameless and at peace with him" (2 Peter 3:14 NIV).

Today, do whatever it takes to have that peace. If you need to ask someone's forgiveness, apologize, or write an encouraging letter, do it! Save the day by deciding to get out of the doldrums instead of wallowing in your feelings and looking for a pity party.

If people around you constantly feel sorry for themselves, complain, sin, gossip, and talk about their illnesses, make a break—get away! You have the support of millions of Christians who have gone on before you: "Therefore, since we are surrounded by such a great cloud of witnesses, let us throw off everything that hinders and the sin that so easily entangles, and let us run with perseverance the race marked out for us" (Heb. 12:1 NIV). The race before us is to live the abundant life. When a bad hour hits, follow Jesus' lead and don't let anything keep you out of God's grace and fellowship. Like a helpless child, turn to God and cry out, "I need you to get me out of this, God! I can't do it alone." Take to heart the directions in James 4:7: "Submit yourselves, then, to God. Resist the devil, and he will flee from you" (NIV). Tell Satan to hit the road.

As Christians we don't have to live in the mud puddles of life. Our old nature accepted depression, anger, and the inability to forgive, but no longer are we burdened by those old, earthly desires. We can say no, following Colossians 3:5: "Put to death, therefore, whatever belongs to your earthly nature" (NIV).

Unlike me, don't wait until you are past forty to realize that God is in the day-salvaging business. Don't let twenty-four hours go to waste because Satan's getting the best of you. Make a decision with God's help to save the day!

35

Don't Sell Yourself Short

Fashion-conscious sex expert Tiamorya Ilori gives advice to her high-school peers and gets paid $5.00 an hour by Planned Parenthood of Menlo Park, California, to hand out free condoms and bring in her friends who want abortions.

"I have a clientele of about eighty students," the sixteen-year-old proudly told the *San Francisco Chronicle*. The school nurse is proud of Tiamorya because she reaches teens adults can't get to.

When I tell this story to some people, they are not shocked. In fact, so few people seem surprised by it that I had to ask myself, "Why do people sell themselves short? Why don't they expect more of themselves and others?"

Our standards have become so low that any mediocre ideal seems to do. People don't seem to reach for greatness anymore. Instead they settle for Satan's lies.

Though Satan can make us settle for something less than God's standards, it doesn't change what is right and wrong. I challenge you to live by the standards God has set:

Standards of holiness. God never said, "Hand out condoms since teens will have sex anyway!" Giving in to the pressure to sin is not God's solution to the problem. Instead he calls us to holiness:

> It is God's will that you should be sanctified: that you should avoid sexual immorality; that each of you should learn to control his own body in a way that is holy and honorable, not in passionate lust like the heathen, who do not know God; and that in this matter no one should wrong his brother or take advantage of him. The Lord will punish men for all such sins, as we have already told you and warned you.
>
> 1 Thessalonians 4:3–6 NIV

God offers no compromises, just strong standards to live up to and something exciting to shoot for.

Standards for obedience. God has given us laws to live by, and he won't change them to make it easier on us. "Keep my decrees and laws, for the man who obeys them will live by them. I am the LORD" (Lev. 18:5 NIV). He didn't change the rules for Israel when that nation became full of pride and self-sufficiency:

> You warned them to return to your law, but they became arrogant and disobeyed your commands. They sinned against your ordinances, by which a man will live if he obeys them. Stubbornly they turned their backs on you, became stiff-necked and refused to listen.
>
> Nehemiah 9:29 NIV

Notice that if we want to be happy and in God's graces, we must live by God's rules and standards—we don't get to choose our own. As his creations, we don't have the right to set the rules—he does.

Standards for life. God hates the murder of the unborn. "There are six things which the LORD hates, yes, seven which are an abomination to Him: . . . hands that shed innocent blood" (Prov. 6:16–17). God will always hate the killing of his precious creations because he formed us in our mothers' wombs.

For Thou didst form my inward parts;
Thou didst weave me in my mother's womb.
I will give thanks to Thee, for I am fearfully and won-
derfully made;
Wonderful are Thy works,
And my soul knows it very well.
My frame was not hidden from Thee,
When I was made in secret,
And skillfully wrought in the depths of the earth.
Thine eyes have seen my unformed substance.

Psalm 139:13–16

Today the blood of innocent children cries out to God, just as Abel's did after Cain murdered him. God asked Cain: "What have you done? The voice of your brother's blood is crying to Me from the ground" (Gen. 4:10).

Standards for heaven. God has control over who will inherit his eternal home.

Do you not know that the wicked will not inherit the kingdom of God? Do not be deceived: Neither the sex-ually immoral nor idolaters nor adulterers nor male pros-titutes nor homosexual offenders nor thieves nor the greedy nor drunkards nor slanderers nor swindlers will inherit the kingdom of God.

1 Corinthians 6:9–10 NIV

When you disagree with what God says, you aren't manip-ulating his rules for entry into eternal life; you're setting your-self outside of them. You don't get to rule in heaven—God does.

Don't let the winds of our times blow you around like the leaves in the fall. Don't follow standards of those who can't think for themselves or who constantly change their direction.

You can choose what is right. Don't sell yourself short.

36
Don't Settle for Less

She'd had sex with three different boys over the last two years. "They said they loved me and would never leave me," this eleventh-grader sobbed. Instead, each one had used her and then left her in the dust of her confusion and hurt.

"Cindy, why are you settling for less than God's best for you?" I asked.

She looked even more confused, seeming not to have a clue what I was talking about.

"God's love for you is the most awesome love you'll ever know," I explained. "What you've been doing is wrong, and you are separated from God by that sin. But it doesn't have to be that way. Turn your back on your sins and accept his forgiveness, and God will give you a new life."

I told her what that new life would mean. "Being saved from your sins means you have an intimate relationship with God. You'll be closer to him than to any boy who has promised you he'd never leave.

"God will help you make the right choices in life, if you trust him and obey his commands," I continued. "He'll give you the ability to avoid doing things that would break the friendship between you, because you'll want to please him more than yourself. You'll start saving yourself for your husband.

"If we do things his way, God protects us from the consequences of sin. When we let him guide us, he provides for all our needs," I promised.

It would have been better if Cindy had never settled for less than the best. She could have been free from the guilt, shame, and low self-worth that accompany premarital sex. Though she may not feel them much now, those may stop her in her tracks years later. Her heart and mind may have a hard time erasing the memories of the scars of her sin. Hurt remains because she knows that she gave herself to guys who were only having fun at her expense.

God's love for you is the most awesome love you'll ever know.

If you've made Cindy's mistake, put a stop to the pain today by trusting in God and obeying him. If you have not made Cindy's mistake, continue to say no to premarital sex. When the guy you're dating asks why, point out these built-in benefits to your stand:

- You will never have to compromise from God's high standards.
- Your purity will make you even more beautiful.
- You'll find it easier to be honest with yourself because you are being honest with God.
- When real love comes along, you will know it because God's standards will help you identify counterfeits.
- You will be a whole, healthy person—not someone who doesn't love who she is and what she stands for.
- You'll find it easier to be loyal to your spouse because you've learned to control yourself now.
- You will value people, not use them.
- You will see to it that your dating relationships glorify God.

- You will learn to show love in many ways, not just sexually or in intimate, physical ways.
- You will learn to communicate and get to know others better because you will have to date creatively instead of letting your hormones dictate the direction of your fun.

"If the benefits of avoiding premarital sex are so great, why do people fall into having sex?" Cindy wanted to know.

"The world has a way of fooling us when it comes to what's best for us. Satan tries to confuse us and control our minds when it comes to looking for real love and not settling for fake love," I told her.

I've asked teens why they settled for *any* love, rather than *real* love, even though they were sure they'd get hurt. Here are some of the reasons they shared with me:

Attention. "I knew he just wanted my body," one fifteen-year-old shared, "but it felt good to be noticed." Because she felt emotionally empty, this teen was willing to go with anyone who would fill that need—even temporarily. That choice only led her to a lot of hurt.

Why do teens settle for pain and heartache when joy is free? Why do they let Hollywood set their agenda instead of God? God was here first, and he tells us that by obeying him, we will never have to look over our shoulders and wonder whom we lied to or when our latest sin will find us out.

That's the kind of notice no one needs.

Fitting in. Many people feel the pain of being popular at all costs. Teens may spend lots of hours wishing they were someone else. But because they can't really be someone else, they pretend. Attempts to fit in with a different crowd or longings to date a certain someone fill their days. The *if onlys* consume them: "If only I lived someplace else, I'd be happy." "If only I had her looks or talent, I could be myself." "If only I was older . . . could drive . . . had green hair. . . ." What a waste of time it is to live in *if only* land.

Cheated childhood. When children are mistreated, they often grow into teens who feel they have the right to treat others the way they've been treated. "Why should I respect others?" they ask. "No one ever treated me that way."

Such teens are angry at God and the rest of the world. Perhaps they've been abused or raped, and their deep pain at being cheated of a childhood erupts in actions that show their hurts.

God is dead. Seeing true love and compassion acted out may convince you that God loves and cares for you. But to many teens, God is no more concerned about them than the adults who hurt them. When God seems not to exist and hate is all a person sees, it's easy to see why he or she would find *right* and *wrong* dirty words.

God is and always will be alive. No matter what sins you, your family, or your friends have committed, he has enough love to cover them. He wants to be your best friend and personal Savior. With him at your side, you can travel through these difficult years without picking up the scars that sin causes.

God has only the best for you. I hope that Cindy has discovered that in her own life. I hope that she will take the time to look into God's Word and discover the following verses:

> Do you not know? Have you not heard?
> The LORD is the everlasting God, the Creator of the
>   ends of the earth.
> He will not grow tired or weary, and his understand-
>   ing no one can fathom.
> He gives strength to the weary and increases the power
>   of the weak.
>
> Isaiah 40:28–30 NIV

Those are power-packed words. God is alive. He created you and the universe—he will always be God. The world may change, but not him. Get to know and trust him. He'll never let you down. He'll be your strength to do what's right.

God doesn't want you to feel the punishment that comes with an immoral lifestyle, but if you turn your back on him, that's what you will be earning. So don't get the kind of wages you don't want—get the blessings God holds for those who obey him.

37
No More Shame

"It was all my fault," Tara said. "If only I had been a better daughter, my parents might still be married today." Shame gripped this teen at the thought that her parents had split up while she was in junior high.

"Tara, children don't cause divorces," I explained. "What you are feeling is shame. But this is one case when you didn't do anything wrong. You couldn't have changed it, and you shouldn't accept the blame."

Shame can cripple a Christian's walk—especially if it is undeserved shame. We feel shame when we know we've done something wrong or we should have done something and didn't do it.

The problem is that sometimes people try to make us feel guilty for something we didn't do—as in Tara's case. Tara's mom felt so much pain that she took it out on her daughter, telling her it was all her fault. Her mom may have felt bad as soon as the words were out, but she never said "I'm sorry" to her daughter. For years Tara had carried that pain.

You can't control what others have done, but you can turn back the guilt when you realize that they are taking out their hurt on you. You can also take control of your actions by daily living out this challenge from the apostle Paul: "For I live in eager expectation and hope that I will never do anything that will cause me to be ashamed of myself" (Phil. 1:20 TLB).

Everyone has at least one weak area that Satan works on to destroy her walk with God. Identify yours by seeing what keeps getting the best of you. Inventory your past failings, and see if there is a spot you haven't noticed before. Are you hiding a secret sin you think no one knows about? If so, you probably feel as if you enjoy it too much to give it up, and you keep finding ways to justify it. But God knows, and you know he knows, so you feel the shame.

Deep in your heart and conscience you know what is pleasing to God and what causes him pain and sorrow. But it's easy to look at the rest of the world and excuse yourself on the grounds that others, who don't know him, are a hundred times worse than you. "Just this once," you argue with yourself, before you give in to that temptation. Afterwards you feel guilty and plead with God to forgive you, but as soon as the heat is off, the pleasure tempts you again. So you keep on sinning.

The good news is that you don't have to keep falling into Satan's trap. I challenge you to stay away from anything that could cause you to be ashamed of your actions.

"That would mean I'd have to go live on Mars," Tara objected.

Choose today to please God with every thought, word, and action.

"You can do it if you focus on Jesus today," I answered. "If your heart and mind are on him, sin will be repelled from your life. It will be like oil hitting water or two same-pole magnets pushing hard to get away from each other.

"You own your actions, and you must live with the shame of the wrong ones. Choose today to please God with every thought, word, and action. Tonight when you go to bed, God will say, 'I'm proud of how you lived for me today.'

"Go have a great day in the name of Jesus," I challenged her, "one with no more shame."

38
I Just Love That Show

Having a sense of belonging, knowing that right is still right and wrong will always be wrong, and seeing a lifestyle in which Mom, Dad, Grandpa, Grandma, and all the brothers and sisters are around is such fun. I think that's why I cherish the show *The Waltons* so much. Every episode taught character, and the family protected and loved one another. Though they made their share of mistakes, they were not too proud to apologize or ask forgiveness.

John Boy challenged me to choose my words with care and precision and to never treat my writing flippantly. The family's lifestyle reminded me that simplicity in one's world is really more, not less: They had more freedom to smell the fresh morning mist or to mourn the death of the family cow, remembering all the babies that were raised on its milk. There was freedom to be oneself with little pressure from the media, since radio was the thrill of the day.

I loved to see the family eating together, and John Walton using a thundering but gentle hand to discipline one of his disobedient children. Afterward he would sit with his protective arm around the child, reminding him or her what the Walton name means and encouraging the child never to forget that respect and integrity are pursued and expected in the Walton household. On one show, John told John Boy that if he wouldn't run a race for fun, but merely to prove he was better than a bragging, big-mouthed rival, then he shouldn't run the race at all.

I liked hearing Jim Bob and Mary Ellen saying, "Yes, Daddy," "No, thank you, Mama," "I love you, Grandma," or, "Thanks for helping, Grandpa."

Why did those shows make me want to cry? Because I didn't have a childhood like that, and I'm pretty sure you didn't either. If you did, thank your heavenly Father and your earthly parents because you are deeply blessed.

I want to make my house into a warm, tradition-filled home. When neighbors and friends visit, I want them to enter a home full of patience, gentleness, and consistent harmony because I live out those qualities instead of just writing about them. I don't want my children to be afraid of my response if they ask for something or confess a wrongdoing. I want to make sure I do nothing wrong so I can look my God right in the eye and not be ashamed of who I am.

Just like the Waltons, I want to save some energy for the end of the day, but I want to do more than say, "Good night, Mary Ellen. Good night, Elizabeth. See you in the morning, Ben." Instead I'd like to pray with my kids so that they know I love them and their Creator with all my heart. I want to lie on their beds and listen to their thrills and spills of the day and hear about all their dreams and schemes.

Friends—that's what I most want to be with Holly and my three beautiful miracles. Maybe the Waltons' example will help me in my struggle to achieve that. But the peace I'm really looking for won't come by turning back the clock. Even if I could live in the Waltons' age, I wouldn't necessarily have it all together.

I can have a peace-filled existence, though, by trusting in God, who promises, "The steadfast of mind Thou wilt keep in perfect peace, because he trusts in Thee" (Isa. 26:3).

39

Painfully Shy

"People at school think I'm a snob because I don't make eye contact in the halls. They ask me to go with them and do fun stuff, but I almost always say I have something else to do. I am so shy that I'm afraid to speak up and be myself. The pain is horrible. I can't talk to people or even ask a question in class," Dierdre lamented.

"Being shy and sensitive are things you are born with. God made you that way," I comforted her. "But being afraid of people and life is another matter altogether."

Some of the ideas I shared with Dierdre could help you if you have a hard time looking people in the eye and making friends.

"God can help you gain confidence, if you will let him," I told Dierdre. "Most of the world doesn't know this secret about gaining confidence: Put your faith in God, not yourself, and you will become more confident. Faith in God, who has such awesome power, gives you the security and courage you lack. Looking people in the eyes and speaking up in public will become much easier when you understand that you are not alone."

Placing your confidence in God will do more than make you able to talk. "Blessed is the man who trusts in the LORD and whose trust is the LORD" (Jer. 17:7). Once God is your source of strength, you surely won't be afraid of people. It is to him that "we have boldness and confident access through faith in Him [Jesus]" (Eph. 3:12).

Your fear and timidity do not come from God. "For God did not give us a spirit of timidity, but of power, of love, and of self-discipline" (2 Tim. 1:7 NIV). As God fills your heart with the strength to love others and live in peace with them, you will overcome your fears.

"My daughter and wife are shy, and they give our family and this world countless blessings," I told Dierdre. "They teach us how to listen, discern the truth, and hurt with others when they hurt. Without people like you, this world would be a heartless, fast-talking, be-one-up-on-the-next-guy kind of place.

"Love your different personality. Work with God, and you will be able to reach out to others," I encouraged her.

If you're shy, you can still be the person God wants you to be. Don't let a fear of people keep you from sharing the world with others. You, too, have so much to offer.

40
Special Cargo

Guitarist Jimmy A. hand carries his guitars everywhere he goes—on a plane, in the hotel van, or in a car.

"Why do you do that?" I asked.

"This is special cargo," he answered. "It needs to be treated with kid gloves." Then he told me of the financial investment he has in these delicate tools of his trade. Most important, they cannot be replaced in time for an engagement. "If something were to happen to this baby an hour before I went on stage, I wouldn't be able to do what God wants me to do with my talents," Jimmy pointed out.

I started thinking about what Jimmy said. Guitars aren't the only things we need to treat with kid gloves instead of tossing them into the luggage rack of life. We need to treat some everyday relationships carefully:

Do you treat God with TLC? Does he go with you when you travel? At school, is he riding in your backpack? Or do you save God for times of desperate need? Do you try to be his best friend for a week during final exams? Do you only know him when you're complaining about not being tall and beautiful or about the fact that you don't have a date for Saturday night? Do you talk of God with disgust or love? Does he get last place or the highest priority in your life?

How about people? Are they really more important to you than things? Do you toss them around every day and only speak nicely to them when you need something? Can you only hug your sister when she's coming off a plane after a long absence?

Airport reunions always amaze me because they bring out the best in folks. People are not afraid to slobber over the young man who is going into the service or has just been discharged. When a boyfriend and girlfriend, husband and wife, or an engaged couple hug after a long absence, people gather around to watch them embrace for thirty or forty minutes. I love it when naturally shy people come out of their shells and give big bear hugs. Then they put their hands on Mom's shoulders and say, "I love you. I'll miss you. I'll pray for you. Come back soon."

Treat people as if they just came back from a four-month absence and you never thought you'd see them again. Or act as if they'd just received a cure for an incurable disease, and now their life has been given back to you again. People really are more important than things!

What of your dreams? Do you handle them with kid gloves? Do you reach for the goals God has placed on your heart? Or do you toss them out the window when you meet with the least bit of resistance?

When God has placed a desire in your heart, what do you do? Do you mold and shape it and find out what you must do to achieve your goal? Or do you toss it aside the moment it becomes inconvenient?

Don't take your dreams or abilities for granted. Develop them and use them to achieve the purpose God has for your life.

Though it would take more money than I'd care to spend, Jimmy A.'s guitar can be bought. It's a tool that he uses to carve out music, and with it he can set your soul on fire. He cares for his tool because of the goals it can accomplish, not because of the price tag alone.

Are you spending time with things that can be bought, even though they have no life of their own? Do you shine up your car but fail to shine the hopes of other people? Or maybe you spend your time in front of the mirror to look good for others. You change your blouse seven or eight times, spend twenty minutes choosing the perfect belt, and make sure that you pick out just the right jewelry. Then you fuss around with your hair and wonder if you need a haircut. But you don't care how you look before God because you only come to him when you're in trouble.

Things that are bought will fade away. You'll grow out of your favorite blouse, and hairstyles will change. But God, his purposes, and the need for loving other people will not alter.

Don't spend your time on the things the Bible says will rust and be torn apart by moths (see Matt. 6:19–21). Make a list of the people, talents, and dreams God wants you to handle with kid gloves. Then invest your time and energy in them. And while you're at it, don't just toss God in the back of the van.

41
Spread the Word

"What if my best friends are good people, but they don't believe in Jesus? Can I share my faith with them and not lose their friendship, or should I just keep quiet?" asked Karla.

I encouraged her to ask herself a few questions:

- If I died tonight, would I regret not having shared this with my friend?
- Do I truly believe in what I wish I had the courage to share?
- Is fear of rejection the main reason why I keep quiet?
- Do I feel this is the right thing to do?
- Is God tugging at my heart to share my faith?
- Am I ashamed of my relationship with Jesus?
- Am I afraid of being branded "goody-two-shoes, Bible lover"?
- Do I simply need a plan so I can share tactfully?

God understands that sharing your faith is difficult. But he would never stir your heart with a desire to do it if he didn't plan to give you the courage it takes.

A close friend of mine felt God tug at his heart to share about Jesus with a man who was in the hospital with cancer. My friend didn't act on God's prompting, and his friend died. Recently he told me, "I will regret that until the day I die."

Jonah, called to witness to an entire city, ran away and went to sea. But God had him tossed out of the ship during a stormy night. Then he rescued the runaway prophet and gave him another chance. Jonah took it! (For the whole story, turn to the Old Testament Book of Jonah.) But it sure would have been easier if he had done it God's way from the beginning. Don't be like Jonah and avoid doing what God commands. You might not like the consequences!

How can you follow God's will, starting today? Follow two steps.

1. *If you don't walk it, don't talk it.* That doesn't mean you have to achieve instant perfection or that you need to know the Bible inside out before you can share your faith. But many people know you, and if they don't see that you are different because you know Jesus, why would they want to have what you have?

Jesus described the influence you can have on others: "You are the world's light—a city on a hill, glowing in the night for all to see" (Matt. 5:14 TLB). Like a bright, glowing city at night, your actions shine out. Make them the kind you can be proud of, so you will be proud to tell others who gives you your strength and wisdom.

2. *Know what to say—have a plan.* Just a few truths from the Bible can have a powerful impact on a friend's life. You don't need to be able to debate every word of Scripture; just share these truths from the Good News:

God loves you. Share this verse: "For God so loved the world that he gave his one and only Son, that whoever believes in him shall not perish but have eternal life" (John 3:16 NIV).

We have sinned. No one has avoided sinning, so everyone starts out apart from God: "For all have sinned and fall short of the glory of God" (Rom. 3:23). "But the trouble is that your sins have cut you off from God" (Isa. 59:2 TLB).

Jesus died for all of our sins. Share these words of Jesus: "I am the way, and the truth, and the life; no one comes to the

Father, but through Me" (John 14:6). Jesus died to pay the penalty for our sins so we could be forgiven. "He died once for the sins of all us guilty sinners, although he himself was innocent of any sin at any time, that he might bring us safely home to God" (1 Peter 3:18 TLB).

Trust Jesus to forgive all your sins. God wants us to trust in him and become part of his family. "To all who received him, he gave the right to become children of God. All they needed to do was to trust him to save them" (John 1:12 TLB). When you love God, he can give you squeaky-clean thoughts: "Now change your mind and attitude to God and turn to him so he can cleanse away your sins" (Acts 3:19 TLB).

Tell your friend, "You can have a personal relationship with Jesus. Would you like to do that now?" Tell her that all she has to do is say a simple prayer that shows she understands the points you've just shared. If your friend says yes, you could lead her in a prayer like this:

> Dear God, I know my sin has separated me from you. Thank you for having Jesus die on the cross in my place. I'm deeply sorry for my sins, because I know they hurt you and others. Please forgive me for them and come into my life to stay forever. Show me how to live for you. Thank you for giving me eternal life. Amen.

If your friend prays this and really means it, she has eternal life. Assure her of that.

Have you ever prayed that kind of prayer? If not, you can pray it now and settle your salvation once and for all.

Know that you are saved, and live for Jesus. When you know Jesus, even though you may goof up once in a while, you won't lose eternal life. That's why God calls it "eternal life," not just "until-your-next-sin life" or "as-long-as-you-feel-good life." It lasts forever and ever—not just a long time, but for *all* time.

God promises those who have trusted in him, "I will never desert you, nor will I ever forsake you" (Heb. 13:5). That means you can have confidence that you have eternal life. John confirms it, "These things I have written to you who believe in the name of the Son of God, in order that you may know that you have eternal life" (1 John 5:13).

God gives his Holy Spirit to believers to help them live the Christian life. "Let us follow the Holy Spirit's leading in every part of our lives" (Gal. 5:25 TLB). Encourage new believers to look to God for guidance that can help them each day to make the best choices. That way they can keep on growing. "And now just as you trusted Christ to save you, trust him, too, for each day's problems. . . . See that you go on growing in the Lord, and become strong and vigorous" (Col. 2:6–7 TLB).

I hope these steps help you have courage to share Jesus with others. Think about how you feel when you get a new camera, computer, or car. No one needs to give you steps on how to tell other people about what you've received. Use the same enthusiasm in your sharing about Jesus. He makes it clear that our courage to share him is proportional to our belief, and he promises to protect us. He warns: "For whoever is ashamed of Me and My words in this adulterous and sinful generation, the Son of Man will be ashamed of him when He comes in the glory of His Father with the holy angels" (Mark 8:38).

In boldness, humility, and strength, let's never be ashamed to walk and talk our faith.

42

Sure Knowledge

"Would you like to know for sure that if you died today you would go to heaven?" I asked the young woman behind the counter as I checked out of the Holiday Inn.

"Oh, no one knows that for sure!" she replied, amazement filling her eyes.

"What do you mean?"

"You can only try your best and go to church a lot and hope that when it's your time to die God lets you in."

"Would you like to know what God has to say about it?" I asked.

"How can I know that?"

"By looking in the book." I opened a small booklet I carry that has Bible verses on salvation, and we found 1 John 5:13: "These things I have written to you who believe in the name of the Son of God, in order that you may know that you have eternal life."

She read it out loud, and the last words gave her confidence.

"How long is eternity?" I asked.

"Forever."

"What must you do to have eternal life and know it?"

She read the first part again, "Believe in the name of the Son of God."

We looked at Ephesians 2:8–9: "For by grace you have been saved through faith; and that not of yourselves, it is the gift of God; not as a result of works, that no one should boast."

As I left, she held tight to that gospel booklet and said, "It sure is great knowing for sure."

Driving away, I thought, "It sure is!"

43

Temptations

"If life is so great, why am I always tempted to do stuff I get in trouble for?" wondered a sixteen-year-old in juvenile detention. She thought life was out to get her.

Have you ever felt that way? Have you ever wondered why we sometimes want to do more bad things than good ones? When you feel lured to do wrong, you've been shot at by temptation. Let's find out who is firing the gun so we can avoid becoming a casualty or fatality.

Three hunters have a lifelong open hunting season: Satan, other people, and our own desires. The bloodstains of sin can be inflicted on us when we fall prey to any of their bullets.

Satan wants to destroy us. Just as he went after Jesus, he'll take aim at us. "The devil took Him [Jesus] to a very high mountain, and showed Him all the kingdoms of the world, and their glory; and he said to Him, 'All these things will I give You, if You fall down and worship me'" (Matt. 4:8–9). If Satan couldn't resist trying his wiles on Jesus, he will certainly attack us.

Jesus also faced temptations from other people. The Pharisees tried purposely to tempt Jesus (see Mark 8:11). They planned to bring him down, to ruin him. When he never fell to any of their tricks and schemes, they had him murdered.

People around you will tempt you to betray your character, integrity, and potential.

Friends often say:

"Come on, one drink won't matter."

"We're in love. Having sex will only put our feelings into actions. Who could it hurt?"

"Lying to your parents won't bring on the end of the world. The weekend is all planned. One small lie and we're headed for fun."

"Forget about the team. They've never done anything for you. So what if you get caught doing drugs and get kicked off—you probably would never make the college team anyway."

Don't fall victim to their ploys and give in to sin.

Finally, we can be our own worst enemies by tempting ourselves to give in to our sinful lusts and desires. Though we may blame God, saying, "He made me this way," we are dead wrong. God doesn't tempt us:

> Let no one say when he is tempted, "I am being tempted by God"; for God cannot be tempted by evil, and He Himself does not tempt anyone. But each one is tempted when he is carried away and enticed by his own lust. Then when lust has conceived, it gives birth to sin; and when sin is accomplished, it brings forth death.
>
> James 1:13–15

Our own desires to please ourselves get carried away, and we give in to them. Then we are one step closer to giving in to Satan's temptation to sin and please him.

What are the results? Lust leads to sin, and sin brings death. All sin causes death of fellowship with Jesus. That's why God gave us a solution to the sin problem: "If we confess our sins, He is faithful and righteous to forgive us our sins and to cleanse us from all unrighteousness" (1 John 1:9).

- Sin brings death to relationships—ask any high-school girl who has given in to her boyfriend's demand for sex, only to be dumped the next day.
- Sin kills hope—ask any drug addict or alcoholic.
- Sin takes away freedom—ask anyone who has to live behind bars because of the wrong he's committed.

In Scripture *death* means separation from the purpose for which God created us. Don't let Satan make you one of the lifeless trophies on his wall. Instead of following along when you know something is wrong, fight back. If you know Jesus and are reading his Word, you know what is right and can turn from the wrong to the right!

44

Throwaway Love

A little girl who wanted to show her love for her daddy thought she would make him a valentine, even though it was just an ordinary day. "My daddy will love this," she thought as she worked on it. She placed the finished card on his dresser so he would see it when he walked into his bedroom.

After school, she ran to his room to see if he had read it. She found it in the wastebasket. Thinking he had accidently knocked it in there, she placed it on his dresser again.

The next evening she found it wrinkled up in the middle of other papers in the wastebasket. She was heartbroken. Then her dad called her to him and said, "Would you quit putting that card in my room? I already know you love me."

What cruel words those were to a child who only wanted to show her daddy how much she loved him. Her father didn't just throw her card in the wastebasket; with those words, he threw her love away.

Your dad may never have been so unkind, but you've probably done something for someone and had him throw it in the trash or into the dirt of thanklessness. Not being loved, appreciated, or thanked hurts.

Small as our love for him might be, Jesus never throws our love away. Even when we do to him what that dad did to his little girl, Jesus loves us. And he sends us the best love letter of all—the Bible.

The amazing thing about God's valentine to us is that it was written with his very life: "But God demonstrates his own love for us in this: While we were still sinners, Christ died for us" (Rom. 5:8 NIV). We are to reproduce that love in our own lives by passing it on to others. "This is how we know what love is: Jesus Christ laid down his life for us. And we ought to lay down our lives for our brothers" (1 John 3:16 NIV).

Though we are often like that father and throw God's love in the wastebasket, though we forget to thank him for his love, he will never be farther from us than a simple prayer. Even if you hate God, he will never stop loving you.

On days when I don't much like myself, I get great encouragement from Paul's words:

> For I am convinced that neither death nor life, neither angels nor demons, neither the present nor the future, nor any powers, neither height nor depth, nor anything else in all creation, will be able to separate us from the love of God that is in Christ Jesus our Lord.
>
> Romans 8:38–39 NIV

Don't tactlessly throw anyone's love in the wastebasket. But be especially mindful of God's love. His love can change your life.

45

It's a Tie

In a rally, speaker Joseph Jennings told thirteen thousand young people that they get to break the tie. You see, God has already voted for you, and Satan has cast a vote against you. But you get to make the tie-breaking vote. Only you can decide who will control your life.

God wants all of you—your heart, will, desires, and hopes. He wants you so much that he gave the most precious thing he owned—the life of his one and only Son, Jesus.

If you have never made your vote for Jesus, Satan has you. And he wants to keep your heart, will, desires, and hopes. Instead of giving you anything good, Satan will take all you have to offer and repay you with lies, deceit, and distortion of the truth. Ultimately he will ruin your life.

There's absolutely no comparison between living for God and living for Satan. I know, because I've tried them both. For the first twenty-eight years of my life, I followed Satan, and he destroyed my life. For the last seventeen years, I've walked with God, and he's rebuilt my life and blessed me so much that I can't imagine wanting to live any other way.

It seems that almost any halfway intelligent person would eagerly swap Satan's lies and the resulting worry and death for the eternal peace, hope, and love God offers. But you must make your own choice. God doesn't force you to choose him. He won't pressure you every day until you give in. He only waits patiently outside the door of your heart: "Behold I stand at the door and knock; if anyone hears My voice and opens the door, I will come in to him, and will dine with him, and he with Me" (Rev. 3:20). Only you can open your heart when he knocks. The doorknob is only on the inside.

"I've made a choice to follow Jesus," you may be saying, thinking back to the time when you were five or when you were in Sunday school and made a decision in the fifth grade.

Have you been living like a Christian? Does your faith show? If you were taken to court on charges that you were a Christian, could your actions convict you of your faith?

**Only you can decide
who will control your life.**

Imagine that a jury sat before you, and the prosecutor brought some of your classmates to the stand and asked, "Did this person act like a Christian?" Could they answer, "Yes, she was loving and caring when everyone else turned their backs on me"? Or could a friend say, "She prayed for me and my family and visited my grandmother when she was in the hospital"? Could anyone say that you had talked about the time you asked Jesus into your life and encouraged her to accept Jesus too? Could half the class report that you prayed in the cafeteria before you ate?

Vote for Jesus and turn from Satan by doing three things:

1. *Give your life to the Lord.* Put your whole faith in Jesus, and you will have new life in him. "If you confess with your mouth Jesus as Lord, and believe in your heart that God raised Him from the dead, you shall be saved" (Rom. 10:9). "He who has the Son has the life; he who does not have the Son of God does not have the life" (1 John 5:12).

2. *Live daily for Jesus.* Once you have Jesus in your heart, you'll change your lifestyle. The things that please him will

come first: "Walk in a manner worthy of the Lord, to please Him in all respects, bearing fruit in every good work and increasing in the knowledge of God" (Col. 1:10). That's how people will know you are a Christian: "You will know them by their fruits" (Matt. 7:16).

3. *Tell Satan to get out of your face and your life.* Tell your friends you will be daily casting your vote for God and his will for your life. Then follow him.

Be ready for the challenges that will follow. When Peter tempted him to turn from the cross, Jesus knew where the temptation came from and answered: "Get behind Me, Satan! You are a stumbling block to Me, for you are not setting your mind on God's interests, but man's" (Matt. 16:23). When friends try to change your mind and keep you from following Jesus, understand that the temptation comes from Satan and don't join in.

As you live for Jesus, automatically God will use you to destroy Satan: "I want you to be wise in what is good, and innocent in what is evil. And the God of peace will soon crush Satan under your feet" (Rom. 16:19–20).

> Live today in such a way
> not as to ask "Why?"
> But live today in such a way
> to say "I break the tie!"

46

No One Told Us Yet

In a Christmas program called "An Old-Fashioned Christmas," we were allowed to eavesdrop on the diary of a twelve-year-old girl who lived during the 1800s. She shared how wonderful the Christmas season was and told us she looked forward to ordinary things such as a big, red apple in her stocking and new socks. She was almost beside herself at the thought that her dad had enough money this year for hard candy.

Grandpa gathered the whole family around him and read the story of Mary and Joseph looking for a place to stay in Bethlehem and finding the stable. With the shepherds the girl's family heard the news of the Savior's birth. Then everyone in the family gathered around to sing "Silent Night," "O Little Town of Bethlehem," "Away in a Manger," "We Three Kings," and other favorites that told of the real meaning of Jesus' birth.

The little girl followed by writing a letter to Jesus telling him how thankful she was that he had loved us enough to leave paradise and come to earth. While he was here he lived among us, teaching us the important things in life, and finally he died on the cross for our sins.

This girl was not upset that she wasn't going to get the latest fashion or toy or game. She was glad to be alive and have her grandparents nearby. Her family worked together, and life was simpler than it is today.

She never had her ears bombarded with ads telling her of all the things she just had to have to make her be noticed, feel good about herself, or to succeed in the world.

At the end of the program, the narrator told of a survey done among some of today's elementary-school children who lived in one of our large cities. Asked "What Christmas songs do you know?" they answered, "Rudolph the Red-Nosed Reindeer," "Frosty the Snowman," and "We Wish You a Merry Christmas." While these songs are lots of fun, they fall short of describing Christ's birth.

Asked "What does Christmas mean to you?" they replied, "Toys, trees, and more toys." On and on went their answers about the things that made them happy: vacation from school, toys, going on vacations, toys, sleeping in, and—you guessed it—toys.

When asked what the true meaning of Christmas was, one boy pitifully responded, "Why, I don't know. No one has told us yet."

How sad to go through life never knowing about our heavenly Father's love. How awful never to know that he allows us to become perfect in his sight when we trust in his Son, Jesus, for our eternal salvation. Without the assurance of knowing you have eternal life, this world can be scary and confusing. I know that, because for twenty-eight years I lived my own way, serving only myself. Today I have hope because someone shared Jesus with me.

One day, that hope lay innocently in a manger. If you see that little boy, please tell him for me so he knows the real story!

47
Which One Are You?

Darrin Harvey's mom was late picking him up, so he began to walk the mile to a relative's house. In the subzero weather, with a wind chill in the negative twenties or thirties, he walked as far as he could. Finally, totally exhausted, and suffering from frostbite and hypothermia, Darrin fell face-first into a snowbank.

An ordinary man, Rush Yarnell, saw the nine-year-old and stopped to pick him up. By the time Rush arrived, Darrin was nearly frozen. But he is alive today because this man cared enough to help him.

Darrin's story appeared in *USA Today* on the same day the paper told of Stella Blizerian, a sixty-nine-year-old who was trying to enter her own front door. Stymied by the frozen lock, she went to her neighbor's house and began banging on the door. Though Stella knew someone was home, no one answered. Her neighbor heard the pounding but was afraid to answer the door. Instead she called 911. But it took over an hour for the crew to arrive, and Stella froze to death.

"I feel bad that she died all alone," the neighbor commented, "but you can't take chances these days. I told the police that if it had happened ten years ago, I would have opened the door."

Which of these people are you most like—Darrin or Stella? When you were out in the cold, were you brought into a warm environment by a loving, caring, protective family? Or are you confused, scared, and angry because abusive things have happened to you? Do you feel the love and compassion of a God who saved you from your sins and is helping you reach your life's dream? Or do you wonder why God has allowed your parents to divorce or allowed you to contract a life-threatening illness?

If you've been blessed with a healthy picture of life because you've had the support of a strong family, thank God and never become complacent. Daily let him know you appreciate all he's given you, and don't take life or the people around you for granted.

But even if you don't have it good now, don't give in to complaints and depression. Whether we have it good or bad, we need to take Job's outlook on life. Even when he lost everything except his wife and his own life, Job stayed pure and did not sin. How could he avoid cursing God? Because his troubles didn't own him. Job was God's and God's alone.

Don't base your happiness on your family or fortune. Like Job, who had been wealthy in his property and relationships, understand that these blessings are on loan to you. "Naked I came from my mother's womb, and naked I will depart. The LORD gave and the LORD has taken away; may the name of the LORD be praised" (Job 1:21 NIV).

Nor should you let sorrow own you. If life's been a dirty deal for you, consider the fact that letting Satan have this victory over you will allow him to ruin you. You may become hard to goodness or stay angry for many years.

Job's wife couldn't see the big picture Job saw. The awful circumstances that hit her family made her bitter. She asked her husband, "Are you still holding on to your integrity? Curse God and die" (Job 2:9 NIV).

Job knew that life is a marathon, not a sprint. How we finish is more important than criticizing the journey. "You are talking like a foolish woman. Shall we accept good from God, and not trouble?" he responded to his wife. And the Bible says, "In all this, Job did not sin in what he said" (Job 2:10 NIV).

When you look at the people who need help, are you like Rush Yarnell? Do you look for people who are lost in the snowbanks of life? They may be too weak to cry out, and if you don't make extra effort, you may never even see them.

You may be surrounded by thousands of people in need. They may not ask for help because they don't think they are important enough for you to bother with them. Perhaps it's the thirteen-year-old who has heard so often that he will end up in jail that it seems inevitable. Like Darrin Harvey, that youngster lies facedown in a snowbank.

Can you hear the knocking of a Stella Blizerian? If you don't respond, she may die. It may be the girl who told you about her problem with alcohol and made you promise not to tell anyone. By not getting her help, you are actually betraying someone who trusted you enough to share with you. She cries out for help but fears that she's beyond redemption. Getting her the solutions she needs shows her that she has a future.

Reach out to others. Show them Jesus in action by bringing them the truth about your Lord and Savior. Meet their needs by bringing them out of the cold, careless world. Even though it's not subzero outside, you may be saving a life.

48

Don't Stop Being Weird

Christians have been called all sorts of things:

- old-fashioned
- out-of-date
- obsolete
- behind the times
- archaic
- weird
- square
- puppets
- people who can't think for themselves

Being a Christian isn't always popular. It certainly isn't politically correct. But I hope I never stop being politically *incorrect,* if that is what it takes to please God. He said: "You adulterous people, don't you know that friendship with the world is hatred toward God?" (James 4:4 NIV). So it doesn't matter to me if I avoid some of the "fun" things in this world. If pleasures get me in trouble with him, they aren't worth the price.

When we stand up for him, we shouldn't expect to be popular. After all, we'll be following in Jesus' footsteps.

If the world hates you, keep in mind that it hated me first. If you belonged to the world, it would love you as its own. As it is, you do not belong to the world, but I have chosen you out of the world. That is why the world hates you. Remember the words I spoke to you: "No servant is greater than his master." If they persecuted me, they will persecute you also. . . . They will treat you this way because of my name, for they do not know the One who sent me.

John 15:18–21 NIV

When I read those words, I can't help thinking of megastars like Madonna, Prince, and Metallica. They seem to defy everything God stands for, and the world loves them as its own.

If the world calls me old-fashioned or weird for following Jesus, I hope it never stops. I've made a list of a lot of things I hope I never stop doing in his name.

- Being angry at the murder of unborn babies made in God's image.
- Getting upset and sick when I hear about abuse of any kind, perpetrated by anyone.
- Waking each day and wanting to get into God's Book to see what he has for me.
- Praying for opportunities to share Jesus with people who don't yet know him as their best friend.
- Recognizing right from wrong.
- Getting mad at the thought of date rape or an angry husband demanding sex from his wife.
- Being called names for being sold out to Jesus.
- Confessing my sins before him, and trusting him to clean out my heart again.
- Telling my children "I'm sorry" and "Will you forgive me?" when I have wronged them.

- Praying for people.
- Loving others the way Jesus wants me to.
- Forgiving others the way God forgave me.
- Carrying my Bible with pride anywhere I go.
- Standing up for God at any time, before any group, whenever I'm speaking.
- Hugging my kids, telling them I love them, and praying for them.
- Finding new, creative ways to show my wife I love her.
- Writing about Jesus and his ways of doing things, even when words are hard to find and it doesn't seem important that day.

Do you prefer to avoid the words that hurt by never taking a stand for Jesus? If so, you've fallen into the world's trap. Though the words the world throws at you hurt for a while, they won't affect you forever. But taking a stand for Jesus has eternal rewards—a heavenly home with God.

Isn't it worth it? When you're walking those streets of gold, the ridicule you've put up with today will look like nothing in comparison.

49

Teens' Will

Even teens need a will. God's will, that is!

Have you ever asked yourself "What's God's will in my life?" Perhaps you've wondered "Where will I be in five years? Whom will I marry, and what will I be doing for a living?"

I hope you have connected those questions with the desire to fulfill God's will in your life. If you've made his will a serious consideration, I'm glad—after all, many people never give God's purpose for their lives a second thought.

Would you like to do what God wants you to do five years from now? If so, this surefire formula can help you do that.

It's simple: To be in God's will five years from now, make sure you are in his will five minutes from now. You can be in his will every five minutes if you ask yourself "How would Jesus do this?" Whether it's cleaning your room or studying for a test, make use of Jesus' example:

- Would he be kind or arrogant when he asked your mom a question?
- Would he be polite or demanding when he talked to your teacher or neighbor?
- Would he use his words to build up others, or would he tell a few dirty jokes?

- Would he avoid the latest miniseries, even though everyone else watched it, or would he go along with the crowd?

What are you going to do—your thing or God's? Will you fulfill your pleasure or his purpose? That's the bottom line.

Susan came up to me after I'd spoken at her school and told me how frustrated and depressed she'd been for the past three months, knowing she was pregnant. "I could have avoided it all if I had done things God's way before I gave in to my boyfriend," she admitted tearfully.

You will never get married for the wrong reasons if you date for the right ones.

Looking for God's will means you can avoid mistakes. You will never get married for the wrong reasons if you date for the right ones. Set your standards, then learn about yourself and the opposite sex, improve your communication skills, and live by the standards you've identified. Learn to respect others and live by God's rules. Do what is right in God's sight, and you will look back on your dating time with no regrets or shame. You will have peace, knowing you showed respect for someone's future husband.

Live for God five minutes at a time, and in five years you will be the person he wants you to be, in the place he wants you to be.

50

Worship Me

"Sometimes we worship false gods—and sometimes those gods are us!" When I heard that truth, it struck me hard. You see, though I know that God says "You may worship no other god than me" (Exod. 20:3 TLB), I have a hard time living it out.

My "other gods" aren't formed out of gold or silver, like the ones in Moses' day. Power isn't much of a temptation, either. No, the god I tend to fall before is *me!* It's as if I mentally shove God off his throne and place myself there.

I saw a sign that read "When you are your own god, everything is permissible." Isn't that the truth! When you become the center of the world, anything goes. Fall into this self-centered trap, and you'll never even have to mention it to your friends and family. Your actions will shout "The world revolves around me!" clearer than any words.

Like me, maybe you've sometimes fallen into the trap of believing you are so unique and special that others should notice you all the time. I know that deep down I'd love it if all conversation stopped when I entered a room. (After all, I have so much to add to a conversation; it's only fitting that everyone else should forget what they have to say.) When I think that way, I'm worshiping myself!

We spend lots of time preparing our god for the world. We want him or her to look real good—never out of style or out of sight! If others aren't including our god in the latest gossip or trends, we make it our job to see that changes.

It's all a matter of pride—and pride takes so much time. Let's face it, if each of us is our own god, we have to evangelize the world single-handedly. Who else would tell about this god of our own making?

Recently a friend told me of her seventeen-year-old daughter, Angie, who has made herself into her own god. "Getting her to do anything has become a fight. She's gone from being a kind, considerate, helpful child to being the Queen of Sheba," the concerned mom lamented.

"She treats her brothers like dirt and acts as if her dad and I are her enemies. All she has time for is her boyfriend.

"Now Angie's threatening that if she can't choose her own curfew, she'll move out on her own. She seems to think we should bow down to her if she lifts a finger.

"When did the world start revolving around her?"

By making herself into her own god, Angie has begun to destroy the world around her.

Want false gods? God won't stop you. However, he warns that you won't be blessed, and you'll fall into lots of trouble. Look at the nation of Israel. He wouldn't let his beloved nation escape when they turned to other gods. They kept losing God's blessing, and they paid a heavy price for that. Wars and unhappiness followed their waywardness. Angie will pay for her attitudes in lost relationships, pain, and loneliness.

God is not in the robot-making business. Forcing himself on you or making you place him at the center of your world would never be his way. Instead, he allows you to put him there—but it is your choice.

You choose your own god. If you pick Jesus, he offers you freedom. The compulsion to always look good and be noticed by others will have no power over you. No longer having an unpredictable person like you or me running the show means you don't have to please the world.

You're also free to fail. Even if you mess up a thousand times, it's still okay because you aren't your god. By putting Jesus on the throne of your heart, you've already admitted that.

Instead of following the fads, you'll be able to choose your own style. You can be yourself, too, and decide whom you want as your friends. You won't have to make yourself look good, because your focus will have changed. Honoring Jesus and following his path will be your first choice.

Freedom to succeed also comes when you know Jesus. He releases us from the pressure to be perfect, because when we acknowledge that he is the only perfect one, we can breathe easier and not worry about pleasing others.

Can you imagine this kind of freedom? Mary Jane described it with these words: "When I walk to class, I don't feel as if I have to second-guess what people think about me. If the cutest guy doesn't look my way, so what? I don't take it personally. When I don't get a date for Saturday night, I don't sweat it. My friends from church can get together and have a good time. Even if they're all busy, I know I have my best friend of all—Jesus. Spending time with him may not be like having a date—it can be better."

Living in an everything-is-permissible world where you get to call all the shots means you never have much security. The freedom it offers is shaky, like a house built on sinking sand. Building on God's rules provides the deep security of knowing you have a rock-solid foundation. You belong to Jesus, who is in control of the universe. You can leave everything in his hands.

Deciding to follow Jesus allows hurting people to be themselves and admit they need his comfort. Accepting the fact that we are sinners who have been forgiven means we don't have to pretend. Then we can also tap into God's strength, knowing that he is bigger than we are and has enough love for the whole world.

What kind of God would do all that for me? Not one who expected me to keep track of the whole world and constantly make sure I look good. Because he's all-knowing and all-powerful and is everywhere at the same time, he doesn't need my feeble efforts to keep the world in order. He even has control of my life—he is the reason I'm living at all. I can have confidence in that because he even loved me enough to die for me.

Wow! What a God. He put all that on the line for me.

How would your family feel if they knew you didn't have to be the center of attention all the time? They'd probably feel as if you'd just given them a great gift. Friends could also breathe a sigh of relief. God would love to hear it, too, knowing that now you could save your praise and worship for him alone.

If you've had a problem keeping God on the throne, begin to solve it today by confessing it to him. Join me in this prayer:

> Dear God, I'm sorry that I've been trying to take your place. Instead of living so that people see you in me, I spend my time trying to get noticed myself. You and only you are God, and you deserve all my worship and praise.
>
> Lord, you are the most important thing in my life. I want to get to know you more each day. When I read your Book, or see a sunset and know that you created it, or watch someone help her neighbor, I see you.
>
> Help me put you first, others next, and myself last. Please help me to admit my sins and recognize my unworthiness in your presence. Give me a heart like yours to serve my family and friends even when I don't feel like it.
>
> I love you, Lord, and I'm so sorry I don't show it each day. Help me get out of the way and make room for you. Amen.

Don't let a false god lead you away from the Lord you love. You can't divide your loyalty. Jesus said, "No one can serve two masters; for either he will hate the one and love the other, or he will hold to one and despise the other" (Matt. 6:24).

When God is on his throne in your heart, he's at the center of your universe. That's right where he should be!